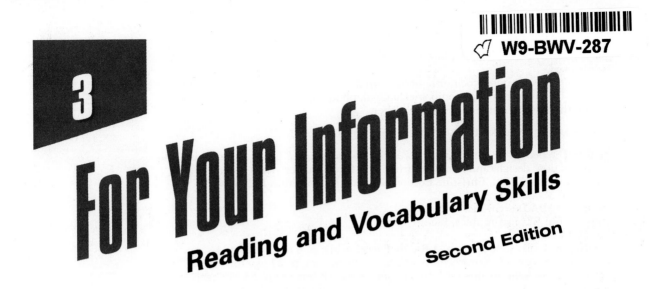

3

For Your Information

Reading and Vocabulary Skills

Second Edition

KAREN BLANCHARD   CHRISTINE ROOT

PEARSON
Longman

For Your Information 3, Second Edition

Pearson Education, 10 Bank Street, White Plains, NY 10606

Staff credits: The people who made up the *For Your Information 3* team, representing editorial, production, design, and manufacturing, are: Rhea Banker, Aerin Csigay, Mindy DePalma, Laura Le Dréan, Christine Edmonds, Linda Moser, Edith Pullman, Pat Wosczyk, and Mykan White.
Cover design: MADA Design, Inc.
Text composition: ElectraGraphics, Inc.
Text font: 11/14 New Aster
Photo credits: p. 1 Christine Root; p. 3 Randy Faris/Corbis; p. 8 no credit; p. 16 Liz Rozin; p. 25 Vladimir Korostyshevskiy/Shutterstock.com; p. 27 age fotostock/SuperStock; p. 34 Yann Arthus-Bertrand/Corbis; p. 42 AP Images; p. 53 Michael Dinges/Getty Images; p. 55 (left) Reuters/Corbis, (right) Albert Ferreira/Reuters/Corbis; p. 56 Ciniglio Lorenzo/Corbis Sygma; p. 61 Stock Montage/SuperStock; p. 78 (left) Royalty-Free/Corbis, (right) David S. Baker/Shutterstock.com; p. 79 (left) Getty Images, (top) Bernard Gotfryd/Getty Images, (bottom) Royalty-Free/Corbis; p. 80 (left top) no credit, (left bottom) Al Freni//Time Life Pictures/Getty Images, (right) Urbano Delvalle//Time Life Pictures/Getty Images; p. 87 Jamil Bittar/Reuters/Corbis; p. 96 Gianni Dagli Orti/Corbis; p. 105 Reuters/Corbis; p. 107 Bettmann/Corbis; p. 116 CBS/Fotofest; p. 123 Reuters/Corbis; p. 149 Jack Novak/SuperStock; p. 150 Robert Holmes/Corbis; p. 159 no credit; p. 161 John McAnulty/Corbis; p. 176 Jodi Cobb/Getty Images; p. 187 Tom & Dee Ann McCarthy/Corbis; p. 189 David McLain/Aurora Photos; p. 196 Larry Williams/Larry Williams and Associates/Corbis; p. 202 Royalty-Free/Corbis.
Text credits: See page viii

Library of Congress Cataloging-in-Publication Data
Blanchard, Karen Lourie
   For your information / Karen Blanchard and Christine Root. — 2nd ed.
    p. cm.
   ISBN 0-13-199186-8 (1 : student book : alk. paper)—ISBN 0-13-199182-5
    (2 : student book : alk. paper)—ISBN 0-13-238008-0 (3 : student book : alk.
    paper)—ISBN 0-13-243694-9 (4 : student book : alk. paper)
   1. English language—Textbooks for foreign speakers. 2. Readers.
I. Root, Christine Baker II. Title.
PE1128.B586 2006
428.6'4—dc22
                                             2006011193

LONGMAN ON THE **WEB**

Longman.com offers online resources for teachers and students. Access our Companion Websites, our online catalog, and our local offices around the world.

Visit us at **longman.com**.

Printed in the United States of America
1 2 3 4 5 6 7 8 9 10—VGH—10 09 08 07 06

This book is dedicated to
our sons, Daniel, Ian, and Matthew,
whose curiosity about the world keeps
them, and us, reading.

CONTENTS

Scope and Sequence

UNIT	CHAPTER	READING SELECTION	READING SKILL
1 **CROSS-CULTURAL CONNECTIONS**	Chapter 1	Kissing Your Way Around the World	Identifying the Main Idea of a Paragraph
	Chapter 2	Communicating with Gestures	Using Background Knowledge
	Chapter 3	The Recipe for Success	Reading with a Purpose
ⓐⓑⓒNEWS **Video Excerpt:** Personal Space			
2 **MYSTERIES FROM THE PAST**	Chapter 1	The Mysterious Statues of Easter Island	Previewing and Predicting Making Inferences
	Chapter 2	The Nazca Lines	Skimming for the Main Idea Making Inferences Scanning for Information
	Chapter 3	Frozen in Time	Reading with a Purpose Making Inferences
ⓐⓑⓒNEWS **Video Excerpt:** Easter Island			
3 **MUSIC TO MY EARS**	Chapter 1	Musicians Who Make a Difference	Using Background Knowledge
	Chapter 2	Happy Birthday to a Musical Genius	Skimming for the Main Idea Identifying Facts and Opinions
	Chapter 3	The Power of Music	Previewing and Predicting Identifying Facts and Opinions Identifying the Main Idea of a Paragraph
ⓐⓑⓒNEWS **Video Excerpt:** Wynton Marsalis			
4 **GETTING DOWN TO BUSINESS**	Chapter 1	The Big Business of Fads	Using Graphic Organizers: Charts
	Chapter 2	The Price of Power	Skimming for the Main Idea Identifying Facts and Opinions
	Chapter 3	Smells Sell!	Using Background Knowledge Identifying Supporting Information
ⓐⓑⓒNEWS **Video Excerpt:** Teen Trends			

VOCABULARY SKILL	APPLICATION SKILL
Learning Synonyms Understanding Word Parts: The Prefixes *il-*, *ir-*, *im-*, and *in-* Understanding Word Parts: The Suffix *-tion*	Reading an Interview Completing a Chart Taking a Survey Writing a Journal Entry
Understanding Word Parts: The Prefix *co-* Learning Antonyms Using Context Clues Understanding Word Parts: The Suffixes *-ian* and *-ist*	Making a Time Capsule Doing Research Writing a Journal Entry
Learning Idioms: Expressions with *Make* Learning Compound Words Learning Synonyms	Making a CD Writing a Journal Entry
Learning Idioms: Expressions about Money and Business Understanding Word Parts: The Suffixes *-able* and *-ible* Using Context Clues Learning Idioms: Expressions with the Word *Smell*	Doing Research Writing a Journal Entry

VOCABULARY SKILL	APPLICATION SKILL
Learning Homonyms	Making a Chart Debating an Issue Taking a Survey Writing a Journal Entry
Understanding Word Parts: The Prefixes *multi-* and *bi-*	
Understanding Word Parts: The Suffixes *-ship* and *-ness*	
Learning Homonyms	Making a Chart Doing Research Writing a Newspaper Story Writing a Journal Entry
Learning Synonyms and Antonyms	
Using Context Clues Learning Synonyms and Antonyms	
Learning Homonyms	Reading a Speech Making a Poster Writing a Journal Entry
Understanding Word Parts: The Prefix *micro-*	
Using *Therefore* and *Because* Learning Synonyms and Antonyms	
Understanding Word Parts: Root Words; The Suffix *-ology*	Making a Poster Reading a Graph Writing a Journal Entry
Learning Idioms: Parts of the Body	
Three-Word Verbs	

The FYI Approach

Welcome to *For Your Information*, a reading- and vocabulary-skill-building series for English-language learners. The FYI series is based on the premise that students are able to read at a higher level of English than they can produce. An important goal of the texts is to help students move beyond passive reading to become active, thoughtful, and confident readers of English.

This popular series is now in its second edition. The book numbers have changed in the new edition and include the following levels:

For Your Information 1	Beginning
For Your Information 2	High-Beginning
For Your Information 3	Intermediate
For Your Information 4	High-Intermediate

Each text in the FYI series is made up of eight thematically based units containing three chapters, which are built around high-interest reading selections with universal appeal. The levels are tailored to focus on the specific needs of students to increase their vocabulary base and build their reading skills. In addition to comprehension and vocabulary practice activities, reading- and vocabulary-building skills are presented throughout each chapter. Although FYI is a reading series, students also practice speaking, listening, and writing throughout the texts. In trademark FYI style, the tasks in all books are varied, accessible, and inviting, and they provide stimuli for frequent interaction.

The Second Edition

The second edition of *For Your Information 3* features:

- new and updated reading selections
- designated target vocabulary words for study and practice
- expanded reading-skill-building activities
- vocabulary-building skills and word-attack activities
- a companion DVD of ABC News excerpts on related themes, with accompanying activities
- a glossary of the target vocabulary words used in the readings

Using FYI 3

UNITS

FYI 3 contains eight units, each with three chapters. Every unit begins
with Points to Ponder questions and concludes with a Tie It All
Together section and a Vocabulary Self-Test.

Points to Ponder

These prereading questions serve to introduce the theme of each unit and
activate students' background knowledge before they delve into each
individual chapter.

CHAPTERS

The basic format for each chapter is as follows:

Before You Read

Each chapter opens with Before You Read, a selection of exercises
designed to prime students for successful completion of the chapter.
Target vocabulary words are previewed here, as are background
questions, activities, and prereading skills such as Predicting and
Reading with a Purpose.

Reading

Each reading relates to the theme of the unit. For variety, the readings
include articles, essays, and interviews. Close attention has been paid to
the level and length of the readings, which range from 600 to 800
words.

After You Read

Readings are followed by a combination of Comprehension Check
questions and activities, along with Vocabulary Practice exercises that
give students the opportunity to work with the target words from the
reading. In addition, throughout this section, the presentation and practice of reading and vocabulary skills encourage students to develop
their
ability to think critically. For example, reading skills such as Identifying
Facts and Opinions, Understanding Cause and Effect, and Making
Inferences are introduced and reinforced throughout the section. Other
activities such as summarizing prepare students to use the information
they gain from reading for writing purposes. Vocabulary skills, such as
Using Context Clues and Understanding Word Parts, are developed
throughout. Talk It Over questions appear regularly, as do culminating
activities that require students to practice real-life skills such as reading

charts, organizing information into charts, taking surveys, and reading Web pages.

UNIT CONCLUSION

Tie It All Together

Each unit concludes with activities that encourage students to think about, distill, and consolidate the information they have absorbed throughout the unit. Among these, Tie It All Together activities are discussion questions based on the general theme of the unit, an activity that is "Just for Fun," plus new activities based on an ABC News excerpt related to the unit theme. This section also features the Reader's Journal, an opportunity for students to reflect, in writing, on the ideas in each unit.

Vocabulary Self-Test

Each unit closes with a vocabulary self-test to help students review new words they've learned. Answers to the self-tests are found at the end of the book.

References

Campbell, Pat. *Teaching Reading to Adults: A Balanced Approach.* Edmonton: Grass Roots Press, 2003.

Drucker, Mary J. "What Reading Teachers Should Know about ESL Learners: Good Teaching Is Teaching for All. These Strategies Will Help English-Language Learners, but They Will Help Typical Learners as Well." *The Reading Teacher*, Vol. 57 (1), September 2003.

Pang, Elizabeth S., and Michael L. Kamil. *Second-Language Issues in Early Literacy and Instruction.* Stanford University: Publication Series No. 1, 2004.

Singhal, Meena. *Teaching Reading to Adult Second Language Learners: Theoretical Foundations, Pedagogical Applications, and Current Issues.* Lowell, MA: The Reading Matrix, 2005.

Text Credits

page 3, Adapted from "Those Crazy Kissing Customs" by Leslie A. Dendy, first published in CRICKET magazine, February 1992, Carus Publishers. © 1992 by Leslie A. Dendy. Reprinted with permission of Leslie A. Dendy; **page 9**, Adapted from *Do's and Taboos Around the World*, by Roger E. Axtell, 3rd Edition, copyright 1985, 1990, 1993 by Parker Pen Company. Published by the Benjamin Company, Inc.; dis-

Bring?" taken from *Witchcraft, Superstition, and Ghostly Magic*. Copyright © 1971 by Daniel Cohen. Used by permission of the Author and his Agents, Henry Morrison, Inc; **page 161**, From COBBLESTONE's August 1989 issue: *Environmentalism* © 1989, Cobblestone Publishing, Inc. 7 School St., Peterborough, NH 03458. Reprinted by permission of the publisher;

page 167, From *Freedom and Culture* by Dorothy Lee. (Englewood Cliffs: Prentice-Hall, 1959), 163ff.; **page 169**, Adapted from "Our Endangered Wildlife." Reprinted by permission, National Geographic WORLD. Copyright February 1990, National Geographic Society; **page 174**, Adapted from "Elephants in Danger" by Cate Dunham from www.kid-snewsroom.

org; **page 176**, Adapted from "The Heat is On! Welcome to Life in the Greenhouse," *Time For Kids*, October 7, 2005, Vol. 11, No. 6. Used with permission from TIME FOR KIDS magazine; **page 189**, Adapted from "Discovering the Secrets to a Long Life" by Martha Pickerill, *Time for Kids*, October 31, 2005. Used with permission from TIME FOR KIDS magazine; **page 196**, Adapted from "What Makes a Champion?" by Joe Lewis. Published in *Parade Magazine*, January 29, 1995. Reprinted with permission from Parade, copyright © 1995, and from the author; **page 202**, "The Surprising Power of the Aging Brain" by Jeffery Kluger, *Time Magazine*, June 16, 2005 and "Brain Power's Sliding Scale" by Judy Foreman. Published in *The Boston Globe*, May 16, 1994; **page 206**, Data from Malmgren, R., in *Textbook of Geriatric Neuropsychiatry*, 2000.

Acknowledgments

We are sincerely grateful to our families for their unending patience and interest in this project and for giving so freely of their time and creative energies. We are also immensely appreciative of the generosity of our friends, colleagues, and students for agreeing to read just one more arti-cle and try out just one more activity.

We acknowledge with thanks the guidance and suggestions of reviewers. Last, but most definitely not least, at Pearson Longman, we thank Anne Boynton-Trigg, Joanne Dresner, and Laura Le Dréan for their faith in us. Thanks are due to Mindy DePalma, Aerin Csigay, and Debbie Sistino for their thoughtful care in the editing process.

We hope that you and your students enjoy the readings and activities in this text and find them interesting *for your information*.

KLB, CBR

About the Authors

Karen Blanchard and Christine Root first met when they were teaching at the University of Pennsylvania. It wasn't long before they began working on their first book, *Ready to Write.* They have continued their successful collaboration, producing more than 17 popular reading and writing textbooks.

Karen has an M.S.Ed. in English Education from the University of Pennsylvania, and Christine has an M.Ed. in English Education from the University of Massachusetts, Boston. Both authors have over twenty-five years' experience working with English-language learners at the university level. Karen has also taught at the American Language Academy at Beaver College, in addition to tutoring students at many levels. Christine has taught in the Harvard ESL program and is a founder, coordinator, and guide in the ESOL tour program at the Museum of Fine Arts, Boston. Karen and Christine continue to enjoy working together to create English-language textbooks for students around the world.

CROSS-CULTURAL CONNECTIONS

Customs, like languages, differ from one culture to another. The way people greet, or say hello to, each other is an example of a custom. The way people prepare food is also a custom. In this unit, you will read about some different kinds of customs around the world.

Points to Ponder

Think about the customs of classroom behavior in your culture. Which statements are true in your country? Check (✔) them. Then discuss your answers in a small group.

- [ ] 1. Students can ask questions during class.
- [ ] 2. Students can eat during class.
- [ ] 3. Students stand up when the teacher enters the classroom.
- [ ] 4. Students call the teacher by his or her first name.
- [ ] 5. Students stand up when they speak in class.
- [ ] 6. Students have discussions in small groups during class.

Kissing Your Way Around the World

Before You Read

A Discuss these questions with a partner.

1. What are the customs for greeting someone in your culture? Do you shake hands? Bow? Kiss?
2. Do you greet older people differently? What about younger people?
3. Do you greet men and women differently?

B Check (✔) the boxes that are true for your culture. Then compare answers as a class.

	Usually	Sometimes	Rarely
1. People kiss to say hello when they meet each other.			
2. Parents kiss their children.			
3. Couples kiss in public places.			
4. People kiss to say good-bye when they leave each other.			

C Learn the meanings of the following words and phrases before you read the article. The numbers in parentheses indicate the paragraph where the word first appears in the article.

vary (2)
associated with (3)
make up (3)
documents (4)
deal (4)
represent (4)
instead of (5)

Kissing Your Way Around the World

by Leslie Dendy

1 What are the customs for kissing people in your country? Do you kiss  your relatives when you visit them? Do you kiss your friends hello when you meet them? Is it polite to kiss someone in public places in your country? All of these kissing customs depend on where in the world you are. Kissing may seem as universal as language, but in fact, kissing customs differ around the world.

2 In many places, kisses are used for saying hello. If you are in Europe or South America, you will see lots of these greeting kisses. But the kissing customs for greeting people vary from country to country, and traveling to new places can be confusing if you don't know them. Many European men and women say hello with two kisses, one on each cheek. But three kisses are polite in Belgium, and young people in Paris often prefer four. In these countries, you *must* start with the right cheek. Starting with your left cheek would be as awkward as sticking out your left hand for a handshake. A variation on the cheek kiss is found in Brazil. When women meet, they put their cheeks together and kiss the air. In some cultures, men kiss each other on the cheeks at business meetings. It's like shaking hands. In some parts of the world, people don't kiss when they meet each other. In fact, kissing in public is considered impolite. In Japan and China, for example, people in public places rarely kiss each other. In most Middle Eastern countries, men and women do not kiss in public, either.

3 Kisses aren't just for saying hello; people kiss for lots of other reasons as well. For example, a kiss can also be a sign of respect. Some people show respect by kissing religious articles and flags. Others kiss the ground when they come home to a country they love. Europeans and Latin Americans also use kisses to say

"beautiful!" They kiss their fingertips when they see a pretty woman, an expensive car, or a great soccer play. In other places, people say good-bye by kissing their fingertips and blowing the kiss away. Kisses are associated with good luck, too. The French started the custom of kissing their cards for good luck before playing, and today, some people kiss a pair of dice before they roll them. The English kissed hurt fingers to make them better, as many mothers still do today. And, of course, people also kiss to make up after a fight.

Kissing Through History

4   Kissing was even more common in the past. In ancient Rome and Greece, for example, people kissed a lot. They kissed family, friends, and even strangers. The Romans sometimes kissed anyone they met on the hand, the cheek, or the mouth. They often put a perfume such as myrrh in their mouths to make the kisses more pleasant. They also kissed the hands, feet, and robes of kings and queens. Students kissed their teachers' hands. During the Middle Ages[1], kisses were used to make a promise. Kings and knights[2] kissed each other in special ceremonies. The knight's kiss was a promise to fight for the king. In return, the king's kiss was a promise to give the knight land and money. In the past, people kissed documents to show that they promised to keep the agreement. Back then, many people couldn't write their names, so they signed papers with an X. The X was their signature. Then they kissed the X to show that they promised to keep the deal. People still use Xs today, but they have nothing to do with promises. Some people like to sign cards and letters with Xs at the bottom. The Xs represent kisses. When you put Xs in your letter, it means you are sending kisses to the person you are writing to.

5   In other places, kissing was not very common at all. In some cultures, for instance, people rubbed their noses together instead of kissing. In Malaysia and Polynesia, people would just put their noses close to each other's faces and sniff. The ancient Egyptians probably did this, too. In fact, in several languages, the word for "kiss" means "smell."

6   Kissing will probably still be around a thousand years from now, but the rules may keep changing. Remember that kissing customs depend on where you are and that in some parts of the world kissing in public places is considered impolite. ■

---

[1] **Middle Ages** – the period in European history between the fifth and fifteenth centuries A.D.

[2] **knight** – in the Middle Ages, a man with a high rank who fought while riding a horse

After You Read

Comprehension Check

A Read these statements. If a statement is true according to the article, write *T* on the line. If it is false, write *F*.

_____F_____ 1. A kiss means the same thing all over the world.

_____ 2. In many places, a kiss is a kind of greeting.

_____ 3. In some countries, it is not polite for people to kiss in public.

_____ 4. In the past, kisses were used to make a promise.

_____ 5. The ancient Romans rarely kissed each other.

_____ 6. Kisses can be a sign of respect.

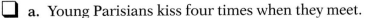

SKILL FOR SUCCESS ✓

Identifying the Main Idea of a Paragraph
Most paragraphs have one main idea. Good readers try to find the **main idea of a paragraph** as they read. Identifying the main idea of a paragraph will help you understand the meaning. Sometimes one sentence of a paragraph (often the first or last) expresses the main idea. Other times, you need to use all of the information in the paragraph to figure out the main idea.

B Check (✔) the statement that expresses the main idea in each group.

1.
☐ a. Young Parisians kiss four times when they meet.
☑ b. Kissing customs for greeting people differ from country to country.
☐ c. Many Europeans say hello with two kisses, one on each cheek.

2.
☐ a. Kisses are also associated with good luck.
☐ b. For example, a kiss can also be a sign of respect.
☐ c. Kisses aren't just for saying hello; people kiss for lots of other reasons as well.

3.
☐ a. Kissing was even more common in the past.
☐ b. In ancient Rome and Greece, for example, people kissed a lot.
☐ c. During the Middle Ages in Europe, kisses were used to make a promise.

4.
☐ a. In some cultures, for instance, people rubbed their noses together instead of kissing.
☐ b. In other places, kissing was not very common at all.
☐ c. In Malaysia and Polynesia, people would just put their noses close to each other's faces and sniff.

Vocabulary Practice

A Match each word or phrase with the correct definition.

Word or Phrase	Definition
___c___ 1. vary	a. connected in your mind with something else
_____ 2. deal	b. to symbolize or stand for
_____ 3. documents	c. to differ
_____ 4. represent	d. to become friends with someone again after an argument
_____ 5. make up	e. an agreement
_____ 6. associated with	f. in place of someone or something
_____ 7. instead of	g. official papers

B Complete each sentence with the correct word or phrase from Exercise A.

1. I heard you had an argument with Eva. Did you ____make up____ yet?

2. Please sign all of these _____.

3. Some people bow or shake hands _____ kissing.

4. I promise to keep the _____ we are making.

5. The meanings of kisses _____ from one culture to another.

6. In some places, a kiss is _____ good luck.

7. The Xs at the bottom of a letter _____ kisses.

SKILL FOR SUCCESS

Learning Synonyms
Synonyms are words that have similar meanings. For example, *vary* and *differ* are synonyms because they mean almost the same thing. Learning synonyms can help you improve your vocabulary.

C Read the paragraph. Find a synonym for each word or phrase in the chart that follows. Write the synonyms in the chart.

Humans are not the only animals that kiss. For instance, chimpanzees sometimes greet each other with little pecks on the cheek. Other times, they give wide-mouthed kisses when they greet another chimp. They also kiss to make up after a fight. When prairie dogs meet, they kiss each other to discover who is a family member and who is a stranger. Fish called "kissing gouramis" press their mouths together like suction cups.

Word	Synonym
1. kisses	*pecks*
2. argument	
3. find out	
4. people	
5. for example	
6. outsider	
7. become friends again	

Talk It Over

From the article, you learned that customs related to kissing vary from culture to culture. The same is true for many other customs. Discuss these questions as a class.

1. *Using names:* When do you call people by their first names? When can you use nicknames?
2. *Tipping:* Is tipping common in your country? Who do you usually tip? How much do you tip?
3. *Being on time:* Is it important to be on time in your culture? Are there some times when it's OK to be late?
4. *Taking off your shoes:* Do you take off your shoes when you enter a home? Is it impolite to keep your shoes on?
5. *Giving gifts:* When do you give gifts? Are there any cultural rules for gift giving? Are some gifts considered inappropriate?

Communicating with Gestures

Before You Read

A Discuss these questions with a partner.

1. Gestures are movements of your hands or head that show what you mean or feel. What are some gestures that are commonly used?
2. How do you think gestures help us communicate?

SKILL FOR SUCCESS

Using Background Knowledge
Before you read, it is a good idea to think about what you already know about the subject. This is called **using background knowledge.** You will understand what you read more easily when you connect the new information in the reading with information that you already know.

B You are going to read about gestures. Check (✓) the statements about this topic that you think are true. Then compare answers with a partner.

☐ 1. People all over the world use gestures to communicate meaning.
☐ 2. Gestures have different meanings in different countries.
☐ 3. Some gestures are impolite.
☐ 4. Gestures are not very important parts of communication.
☐ 5. Misunderstanding gestures can cause confusion.

C Look at the picture of the cover of a book called *Gestures: The Do's and Taboos* of Body Language Around the World*. Discuss the picture on the book cover with a partner.

* **taboos** – behaviors to avoid because society thinks they are offensive

D Learn the meanings of the following words before you read the article.

authority (2)   attractive (item 9)
extensive (2)   ill (item 9)
rude (item 2)   signifies (item 10)
appreciation (item 4) unreliable (item 15)

Communicating with Gestures

1   People around the world use body language and gestures to send specific messages. Understanding the meanings of gestures and body language and being able to use them correctly are important parts of communicating in a foreign country.

2   Roger Axtell is a leading authority on this subject. He spent thirty years traveling and living abroad. During that time, he gained extensive knowledge of the "do's and don'ts" of personal and business interaction. In fact, he has written nine books based on his observations, and two of his best-selling books have been translated into eleven languages. In his books, he explains how misunderstanding gestures and body language can cause confusion and embarrassment and how using gestures incorrectly can get you into trouble. The information in his books has helped many people who are living in or traveling to a different country. Maybe it can help you, too. Here are some excerpts from his books that describe the meanings of some gestures.

1. **Fingers circle.** This is widely accepted as the American "OK" sign, except in Brazil and Germany, where it's considered vulgar or obscene[1]. It is also considered impolite in Greece and Russia, while in Japan, it signifies "money," and in southern France, "zero" or "worthless."

2. **Thumbs up:** In Australia, parts of West Africa, Russia, Iran, Greece, and Sardinia, it is a rude gesture. In other places in the world, such as the United States, it simply means "OK."

3. **Eyelid pull:** In Europe and some Latin American countries, this means "Be alert" or "I am alert."

4. **Ear grasp:** Grasping one's ears is a sign of apology in India. A similar gesture in Brazil—holding the lobe of one's ear between thumb and forefinger—signifies appreciation.

5. **Nose tap:** In England, this means secrecy or confidentiality, as in "Let's keep this between us." On the other hand, in Italy, it is a friendly warning: "Watch out." or "Take care."

6. **Fingertips kiss:** This is common throughout Europe and in many Latin American countries. It connotes "Aah, beautiful!," the subject of which may be anything from a woman or a wine to a Ferrari or a soccer play.

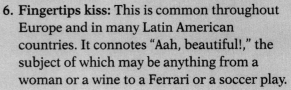

---

[1] **obscene** – offensive and shocking, especially with regard to sexual behavior

7. **Chin flick:** This means "Get lost, you are annoying me." in France and Northern Italy. In Brazil and Paraguay, it signifies "I don't know."

8. **Head circle:** In most European and some Latin American countries, a circular motion of the finger around the ear means "crazy." In the Netherlands and Argentina, it means someone has a telephone call.

9. **Cheek stroke:** In Greece, Italy, and Spain, this means "attractive." In the former Yugoslavia, it means "success." Elsewhere, it can mean "ill" or "thin."

10. **Nose thumb:** One of Europe's most widely known offensive gestures, this signifies disrespect. It may be done double-handed for greater effect.

11. **Head screw:** In Germany, this is a strong symbol meaning "You're crazy." Often used by drivers to comment on the driving skills of other travelers, this gesture can get you arrested! The same gesture is used in Argentina but without the consequences.

12. **Head tap:** In Argentina and Peru, this means "I'm thinking" or "Think." Elsewhere, it can mean "He's crazy."

13. **One-finger point:** Pointing with the index finger is common in North America and Europe. But in most Middle and Far Eastern countries, pointing with the index finger is considered impolite. The open hand is used instead, or, in Indonesia, the thumb.

14. **Hand purse:** This can signify a question or a fear or mean that something is good. It is considered almost the national gesture of Italy.

15. **Elbow tap:** In Holland, this means "He's unreliable."; in Colombia, "You are stingy."

16. **The *wai*:** This is a traditional greeting in Thailand. It is called the *namaste* in India.

17. **Wink:** Winking at women, even to express friendship, is considered improper in Australia.

18. **Nodding and shaking the head:** Throughout most of the world, nodding and shaking the head up and down signifies "yes," and shaking it back and forth means "no." In Bulgaria, however, the custom is just the opposite, especially among older people. There, to signal "no," they nod the head up and down, and to indicate "yes," they shake the head back and forth.

19. **Eye contact:** When greeting and conversing with others, North American children are taught to look others directly in the eyes. To do otherwise is often regarded as a sign of shyness or lack of warmth—or even worse, as weakness. Japanese and Korean parents teach their children to do just the opposite: avert the eyes and avoid direct eye contact. To them, direct eye contact is considered threatening.

20. **Spatial relationships:** In normal situations, North Americans stand about 30 inches (about 0.76 meter) apart from each other. That's considered the personal comfort zone and is equal to about the length of an arm. Asians, however, usually stand farther apart. In contrast, Latin Americans and Middle Easterners stand much closer—sometimes even toe to toe, or side to side, brushing elbows. As a result, North Americans need to be prepared for such close encounters, because to move away would send an unfriendly message.

After You Read

A Read these statements. If a statement is true according to the article, write *T* on the line. If it is false, write *F*.

Researchers estimate that the human hands and face can make hundreds of thousands of different signs and expressions.

_____ 1. Gestures and body language have different meanings around the world.

_____ 2. Asians usually stand farther apart than North Americans.

_____ 3. Many Europeans use the fingertip kiss to mean "beautiful."

_____ 4. Japanese and Korean children usually look other people directly in the eyes.

_____ 5. In most countries, except Australia, the thumbs-up sign means "OK."

_____ 6. The gesture for "OK" has the same meaning in every country.

B Write the name of the gesture you would use in each situation.

1. You are in Italy, and you want to praise someone for doing a good job.
   hand purse

2. You are in Brazil, and your roommate made dinner. You want to show your appreciation.

   _____

3. You are in Latin America at a soccer game. You've just seen your favorite player make the winning goal.

   _____

4. You are in the Netherlands, and you want to show your friend that she has a telephone call.

   _____

5. You are in Thailand at a formal social gathering. The president of your university has just walked in the room. You need to greet him in the traditional way.

   _____

C With a partner, discuss the following situations and answer the questions.

1. You are visiting some friends in Japan, and they introduce you to their ten-year-old daughter. You look her directly in the eyes when you say hello. She looks down and seems worried. Why do you think she may be afraid of you?

2. You are a tourist in Bulgaria. Your host offers you a drink. Since you are very thirsty, you nod your head. You are surprised when your host walks away without giving you a drink. Why did your host ignore your request?

3. You are eating dinner at your Australian friend's house. She asks you if you like her food. You give her the thumbs-up sign. She becomes offended. Why is your friend offended?

Vocabulary Practice

A Match each word with the correct definition.

Word	Definition
_____ 1. authority	**a.** pretty, pleasant to look at
_____ 2. extensive	**b.** sick
_____ 3. appreciation	**c.** to represent or mean something
_____ 4. ill	**d.** containing a lot of information
_____ 5. attractive	**e.** not trustworthy or dependable
_____ 6. rude	**f.** thankfulness for something someone has done for you
_____ 7. signify	**g.** an expert on a subject
_____ 8. unreliable	**h.** not polite

B Answer each question with *Yes* or *No*.

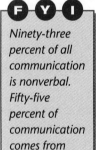

Ninety-three percent of all communication is nonverbal. Fifty-five percent of communication comes from facial gestures.

1. If something is ugly, is it <u>attractive</u>? ___No___
2. If you are an <u>authority</u> on a topic, do you have a lot of knowledge about it? _____
3. Does tapping your head <u>signify</u> "he's crazy" in some places? _____
4. If waving is considered <u>rude</u> in Greece, is it a good idea to wave to a Greek person? _____
5. Would you ask an <u>unreliable</u> person to mail an important letter for you? _____
6. Would you call a doctor if you were feeling very <u>ill</u>? _____
7. Do you show <u>appreciation</u> if someone is rude to you? _____

Understanding Word Parts: The Prefixes *il-, ir-, im-,* and *in-*
A **prefix** is a letter or group of letters that is added to the beginning of a word. A prefix changes the meaning of a word. If you know some common prefixes, it will be easier for you to guess the meanings of some unfamiliar words.

The **prefixes *il-, ir-, im-,*** and ***in-*** mean "no" or "not." They change a word into its opposite. Follow these spelling rules:

- Use *il-* before words starting with *l*.
  not legible = illegible
- Use *ir-* before words starting with *r*.
  not relevant = irrelevant
- Use *im-* before words starting with *m* and *p*.
  not mature = immature
  not perfect = imperfect
- Use *in-* before any other letter.

C Using the prefixes in the chart, write the opposite of each word in the correct box.

possible	appropriate	convenient	responsible
legal	regular	literate	polite

il-	*ir-*	*im-*	*in-*
illiterate			

D Complete each sentence with the correct word from the chart in Exercise C. Use each word only once.

1. Don't drive through the red light. It's dangerous and _____.
2. You shouldn't wear jeans to a formal wedding. It's _____.
3. The little boy doesn't know how to read or write. He is _____.
4. We have no money. It is _____ for us to buy a house.
5. I hope I didn't call you at an _____ time.
6. My brother always forgets to feed his dog. He is _____.
7. In some cultures, it is _____ to wink at someone.
8. Many English verbs are _____. You need to memorize the past-tense forms.

Talk It Over

A Discuss and demonstrate the gesture you would use in each of these situations.

1. to say that someone is crazy
2. to say "Come here."
3. to show that you've got a headache
4. to answer "I don't know."
5. to show that you are annoyed
6. to indicate that someone is cheap
7. to show that something is expensive
8. to say that you can't hear something

B In a small group, discuss the gestures in the chart. Write at least one meaning for each gesture. Then write *Yes* in the last column if the gesture is used in your country or *No* if it is not.

Gesture	Meaning	Is this gesture used in your country?
1. clapping your hands		
2. shrugging your shoulders		
3. snapping your fingers		
4. whistling		
5. winking		
6. crossing your fingers		
7. crossing your heart		

UNIT 1

CHAPTER 3

The Recipe for Success

Before You Read

A Discuss these questions with a partner.

1. How would you describe the typical food from your culture?
2. Do you enjoy eating food from other countries?
3. Do you like to cook? Why or why not? What is your specialty?
4. Have you ever tried to prepare a dish from another country? Did you have any problems?

SKILL FOR SUCCESS

Reading with a Purpose
Reading with a **purpose** means reading with a goal in mind. This will help you become actively involved in the reading process. When you read with a purpose, you will understand and remember information in the text better. You can set a purpose by thinking of some questions that you would like to have answered in the reading. Then, as you read, look for answers to the questions.

B You are going to read an excerpt from an interview with Liz Rozin, a cookbook author and food historian. She has written eight cookbooks on the cultures and foods of the world. Write three questions you hope the interview will answer.

1. _____

2. _____

3. _____

C Learn the meanings of the following words and phrase before you read the article.

cuisine (2)   complicated (6)

system (2)   passed down (6)

flavorings (2)   generation (6)

ethnic (3)

The Recipe for Success

1 **Reporter:** How did you become interested in learning about food from different cultures?

Liz: Twenty-five years ago, my grandmother took me on a trip around the world. I enjoyed trying all the new and different kinds of food. When I got home, I decided to make in my own kitchen some of the foods I had eaten on my trip.

2 **Reporter:** Was it easy to make these foods at home?

Liz: Not at first. Each part of the world has its own special cuisine, or style of cooking. As I tried to create these foods, I began to understand something very important. Just as people have a system for producing language or art, they also have a system for producing cooked food. If I wanted my food to taste like the food I ate on my trip, I had to learn about the special combination of flavorings that each culture uses.

3 **Reporter:** What did you learn?

Liz: The rules and traditions that go into a culture's food depend on three things: the foods that are available, the way the food is cooked, and most importantly, the combination of flavoring. I call these the "flavor principles." Every culture has certain flavorings that it uses over and over. In fact, when I realized that there were systems for preparing ethnic food that could be described and taught, I decided to write my first book, *The Flavor Principle*[1].

4 **Reporter:** Can you explain the Flavor Principle idea?

Liz: OK. Most people want their food to taste good or right. But what tastes good or right to people in one country may seem strange to people from another country. It is the specific combination of flavorings that makes the foods of each culture unique.

5 **Reporter:** Can you give us some examples?

Liz: Sure. For example in Mexico, people use a combination of tomatoes and chili peppers in most cooked food. In Hungary, the combination is onions, fat, and paprika. In Asia, soy sauce is widely used. But among the Asian countries, there are many different combinations used with soy sauce: In China, the combination is soy sauce, rice wine, and

---

[1] **principle** – a rule or a set of ideas that makes you behave in a particular way

ginger root. In Korea, it's soy sauce, sesame, and chili. In Indonesia, it's soy sauce, sugar, and peanuts. In Japan, it's soy sauce, sweet rice wine, and sesame or ginger. As you can see, each culture has its own special combination.

6 **Reporter:** How did cuisines develop historically to become so different?
Liz: Well, it's very complicated. Briefly, cuisines are based on geography, climate, and cultural traditions that are passed down from generation to generation. People like to keep the traditions that have been passed down from their ancestors, and they like to eat familiar foods. What is really interesting is that people might add new foods and new flavors to their diet, but they also keep the old, traditional foods and flavors. ∎

After You Read

Comprehension Check

F Y I

The smell of a food can be responsible for 90 percent of its taste.

A Read these statements. If a statement is true according to the article, write *T* on the line. If it is false, write *F*.

_____ 1. Food that tastes good to one group of people may not taste good to another group of people.

_____ 2. Soy sauce is an important flavoring in many Asian cuisines.

_____ 3. People never add new foods and new flavors to their diet.

_____ 4. Most people like food that is familiar.

_____ 5. Liz Rozin discovered "the flavor principle" in Mexico.

_____ 6. Only a few cultures have a system for producing food.

_____ 7. Cuisines are based on geography, climate, and cultural traditions.

B Complete the chart. Write the correct flavorings used in each country.

Country	Flavorings
1. Mexico	*tomatoes, chili peppers*
2. Hungary	
3. Japan	
4. Korea	
5. Indonesia	

Vocabulary Practice

A Complete each sentence with the correct word or phrase.

complicated	generation
cuisine	passed down
ethnic	system
flavorings	

1. There are many _____ restaurants in most big cities.

2. Each culture combines _____ in a unique way.

3. The way that cuisines have developed is very _____.

4. Each culture has its own _____, or style of cooking.

5. Cultural traditions of all kinds are _____ from one _____ to the next.

6. Do you have a(n) _____ for filing your recipes?

B Ask and answer these questions with a partner.

1. What is your favorite <u>ethnic</u> food?
2. Do you have any recipes that have been <u>passed down</u> from <u>generation</u> to generation in your family?
3. When you cook, what kinds of <u>flavorings</u> do you usually add?
4. Do you have a <u>system</u> for cleaning up the kitchen after you cook?
5. What is the most <u>complicated</u> dish you have ever made?
6. What is your favorite <u>cuisine</u>?

SKILL FOR ✓ SUCCESS

Understanding Word Parts: The Suffix *-tion*
A suffix is a letter or group of letters that is added to the end of a word. Suffixes change the meaning or part of speech of the word.
    Many verbs can be changed into nouns by adding the suffix *-tion*. For example, if you add the suffix *-tion* to the verb *define*, you get the noun *definition*.

C Complete each sentence with the correct word.

1. create   creation
   a. The fashion magazine showed the famous designer's newest _____.

   b. The band members tried to _____ a new kind of music.

2. realize   realization
   a. Do you _____ how important this assignment is?
   b. He came to the _____ that he should change his major.

3. describe   description
   a. The student had to write a _____ of her favorite movie.
   b. Please try to _____ what happened at the meeting.

4. combine   combination
   a. You need to _____ these ingredients before you add the eggs.
   b. Our class is a _____ of people from many countries.

5. complicate   complication
   a. Janet is late. This will _____ our plans.
   b. It didn't happen the way we planned. There was a _____.

Talk It Over

Read the excerpt from a magazine article called "The Global Village Finally Arrives" by Pico Iyer, a famous travel writer. Then discuss the questions in small groups.

The Global Village Finally Arrives

by Pico Iyer

This is a typical day of a relatively typical soul in today's diversified world. I wake up to the sound of my Japanese clock radio, put on a T-shirt sent to me by an uncle in Nigeria, and walk out into the street, past German cars, to my office. Around me are English-language students from Korea, Switzerland, and Argentina—all on this Spanish-named road in this Mediterranean-style town. On TV, I find the news is in Mandarin; today's baseball game is being broadcast in Korean. For lunch, I can walk to a sushi bar, a tandoori palace, a Thai café, or the latest burrito joint (run by an old Japanese lady). Who am I, I sometimes wonder—the son of Indian parents and a British citizen who spends much of his time in Japan (and is therefore—what else?— an American permanent resident)? And where am I?

I am, as it happens, in Southern California, in a quiet, relatively uninternational town, but I could easily be in Vancouver or Sydney or London or Hong Kong. All the world's a rainbow coalition, more and more; the whole world, you might say, is going global. ∎

1. What international references does the author make? Underline them in the text.
2. What do you think Iyer means by, "All the world's a rainbow coalition . . ."? Why does he use the word *rainbow*?
3. Iyer mentions several kinds of ethnic restaurants that are in his neighborhood. What kinds of international restaurants are there in your neighborhood?
4. He also says that several TV programs are broadcast in foreign languages. Is that true in your country? If so, what kinds of shows are broadcast in other languages?

Take a Survey

A *survey* is a list of questions you ask people to find out about their opinions and behaviors. You are going to take a survey about your classmates' cooking habits.

Ask three classmates to answer the questions in the chart. Share your survey results with the whole class.

Questions	Name: _____	Name: _____	Name: _____
1. Do you enjoy cooking?			
2. Do you like to make food from different cultures?			
3. Do you usually follow a recipe when you cook?			
4. Do you ever make up your own recipes?			
5. Do your friends and family think you are a good cook?			

Discussion

Discuss these questions in a small group.

1. Americans have an expression, "When in Rome, do as the Romans do." What do you think this means? Do you agree with the idea? Do you have a similar expression in your language?
2. What other customs (besides the ones discussed in this unit) can you think of from your own culture? Explain them to your classmates.
3. Have you ever had any funny, unusual, or difficult experiences because you misunderstood the gestures or body language of someone from another culture? Share your story with the class.

Just for Fun

Complete the crossword puzzle with words from the unit.

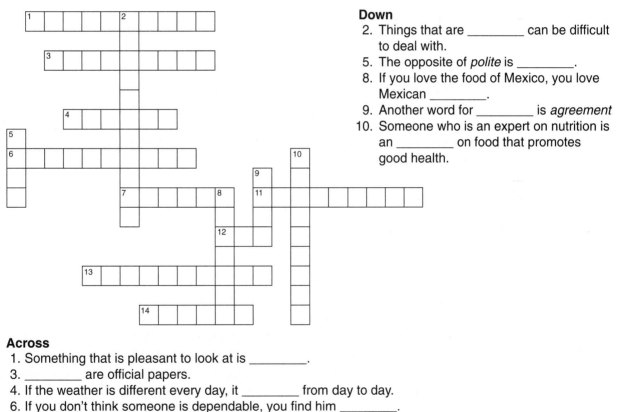

Down

2. Things that are _____ can be difficult to deal with.
5. The opposite of *polite* is _____.
8. If you love the food of Mexico, you love Mexican _____.
9. Another word for _____ is *agreement*
10. Someone who is an expert on nutrition is an _____ on food that promotes good health.

Across

1. Something that is pleasant to look at is _____.
3. _____ are official papers.
4. If the weather is different every day, it _____ from day to day.
6. If you don't think someone is dependable, you find him _____.
7. _____ food refers to the foods of a particular country or culture.
11. Someone who has a lot of knowledge about a certain subject has _____ knowledge of the subject.
12. When you are _____, it's best to stay home and rest.
13. Your grandparents are not in your _____.
14. An organized set of rules or methods used to do something is often referred to as a _____.

Personal Space

Everyone has his or her own personal comfort zone. How far away do you stand from someone when having a conversation? In the video, you will see an interviewer test people's personal comfort zones. Who do you think prefers more distance—people from cities or people who live in open areas?

A Study these words. Then watch the video.

boundaries   invade   unanimously
intimate   philosophy   vast

B Read these sentences. Then watch the video again. Circle the correct answers.

1. Everyone has different _____ of personal space.
   a. voices   b. boundaries   c. emotions
2. Many people feel uncomfortable if their personal space is _____.
   a. considered   b. respected   c. invaded
3. If you sit down near strangers in Arizona, they will probably _____.
   a. be friendly   b. seem unfriendly   c. look shocked
4. A woman from Georgia says people from _____ need more space.
   a. big cities   b. farms   c. suburbs
5. New Yorkers have a personal comfort zone of about _____.
   a. 60 inches   b. 10 inches   c. 25 inches

C Discuss these questions with a partner or in a small group.

1. Do you think it's true that people who live in cities like more distance between them? Give some examples.
2. How do customs about personal space in your culture differ from those you learned about in the video?

Reader's Journal

At the end of every unit, you will write for ten to twenty minutes in the Reader's Journal on pages 221–224. The purpose of the task is to help you think about the ideas in the unit. When you write, don't worry about spelling, grammar, or punctuation. Just try to write as much as you can.

Think about the topics and ideas you have read about and discussed in this unit. Choose a topic and write about it for ten to twenty minutes. You may pick a topic from the following list, choose one of the discussion questions in the unit, or write about a topic of your own.

• an experience you had that involved cross-cultural miscommunication
• a description of the ethnic food in your country
• how gestures help us communicate with others

Vocabulary Self-Test

Complete each sentence with the correct word or phrase.

A associated with   complicated   made up   system
    attractive   ethnic   signify

1. Breaking a mirror is _____ bad luck in some cultures.

2. Janine is a very _____ woman, and she always wears the latest-style clothes.

3. There are many different _____ groups in the United States.

4. Experts say that changes in weather might _____ that pollution is changing our climate.

5. The two sisters had a terrible fight, but now they have _____.

6. Michelle has her own _____ for organizing her e-mail addresses.

7. The questions that she asks me are always too _____. I never know how to answer them.

B cuisine   documents   ill   vary
    deal   generations   unreliable

1. French _____ is one of the most popular in the world.

2. Three _____ of Kemals have lived in this house.

3. Customs for saying hello and good-bye _____ from country to country.

4. My sister was seriously _____, but she is feeling much better now.

5. The two companies have a(n) _____ to work together on a new project.

6. Please sign these _____ before you leave.

7. I don't trust him, and I think his information is _____.

C
appreciation	extensive	instead of	represent
authority	flavorings	pass down	rude

1. I've changed my mind. I'll have the lamb _____ the beef.

2. Dr. Nishimura is a(n) _____ on Japanese art.

3. It was very _____ of him to refuse to shake her hand.

4. Many different _____ go into Chinese cooking.

5. Family members _____ their cultural traditions.

6. I would like to show my _____ for everything my parents have done for me.

7. Doctors have done _____ research into the effects of stress.

8. The green triangles on the map _____ campgrounds.

MYSTERIES FROM THE PAST

The world is full of mysteries. Some of the most fascinating are the amazing creations of people who lived long ago. In this unit, you will read about several of these mysterious creations.

Points to Ponder

Think about these questions and discuss them in a small group.

1. Do you know of any amazing things that ancient people built? Have you ever seen any of them? Which ones would you like to see?

2. Do you believe that there are things in our universe that science cannot explain? If so, give some examples.

3. Are you interested in learning about ancient cultures? Why or why not? What do you think we can learn from studying things that people made and built long ago?

The Mysterious Statues of Easter Island

Before You Read

A Discuss these questions with a partner.

1. Locate Easter Island on the map on pages 218–219. Have you ever heard of Easter Island? If so, what do you know about it?
2. Look at the picture of the statues on page 27. What words would you use to describe them?
3. Are there any mysterious places in your country? If so, what and where are they?

SKILL FOR SUCCESS

Previewing and Predicting
Before they read, good readers **preview** the text and **predict**, or guess, what it will be about. Here's how to do it. First, preview the text by looking it over. Read the title and subtitle, section headings, and words in bold print or italics. Also look at the pictures and read the captions. Doing this will help you predict the content of the reading. Previewing and predicting will help you understand more easily what you read.

B Preview the article by looking at the title, subtitle, headings, and photo. Also read the caption under the photo. Then make predictions by checking (✔) the topics you think will be discussed.

❑ 1. where the statues are located
❑ 2. when the statues were made
❑ 3. the economy of Easter Island
❑ 4. explanations about the mysterious statues
❑ 5. what the statues look like
❑ 6. what archaeologists do
❑ 7. how the statues were raised
❑ 8. how to make your own statue

C Learn the meanings of the following words and phrase before you read the article.

tiny (1)

magnificent (1)

carve (2)

baffled (3)

disasters (5)

figure out (6)

descendant (7)

estimated (9)

silent (10)

cooperated (10)

The Mysterious Statues of Easter Island

by Daniel Pouesi

Stone Statues with Secrets

1 Easter Island is a tiny island in the Pacific Ocean surrounded by 1 million square miles (2.59 million square kilometers) of empty Pacific Ocean. People have lived on Easter Island for hundreds of years. Long ago, the people farmed the land with simple tools. But they also made huge and magnificent stone statues that have puzzled scientists and everyone else for more than two centuries. Why did the islanders build the statues? How did they move them several miles from the places where they were made?

2 There are more than 800 statues on the island. More than 300 of them are unfinished. They are still near the crater[1] of the volcano where they were made. The tools used to carve the statues from the volcanic rock are still there, too. It is as if the workers were called away suddenly and never came back.

The statues of Easter Island

Strange-looking Statues

3 The statues are very strange looking. They have big heads with long ears and noses, square chins, and high foreheads. Their deep-set eyes make them seem old and wise. The largest statue is as tall as a seven-story building and weighs about fifty tons. Think about how

[1] **crater –** the round open top of a volcano

difficult it would be to move it, and you can understand why so many people were baffled.

Where Did the Statues Come From?

4   For many years, people wondered where the mysterious statues came from. At first, some people thought that aliens from outer space had helped make the statues. Other people thought the islanders had magical powers. But none of these explanations really made sense. Then archaeologists began to study the statues, the island, and the people living on Easter Island today.

5   Archaeologists study ancient cultures by examining things people leave behind such as buildings, artwork, pottery, tools, and bones. They use these clues to make inferences about what life in the past was like. Archaeologists usually also talk to people in the area who know something about their ancestors and how they did things in the past. But very few of the people on Easter Island knew about their past. Long before archaeologists came to study the statues, several disasters killed most of the people on the island.

6   In 1955, Thor Heyerdahl, a Norwegian scientist, came to Easter Island with a team of archaeologists. Heyerdahl and his team discovered many things about the ancient people of Easter Island. But he was puzzled by something. He couldn't figure out how the people had raised the heavy statues and put them on their platforms. He wanted to find out.

7   Although very few of the people on Easter Island knew about their past, Heyerdahl found someone who did. That person was the mayor of Easter Island. The mayor was a descendant of one of the island's oldest families. Heyerdahl offered the mayor $100 to raise a statue and put it on a platform. The mayor accepted the challenge.

Solving a Mystery by Raising a Statue

8   The mayor organized a group of men to gather stones and use poles. The poles were pushed under the statue's buried face. Men leaned on the poles to lift the face enough so the mayor could put stones under it. The poles and stones worked as a lever[2]. The men worked for many days. They put more and more stones under the statue. Finally, the statue lay on a huge pile of stones. On the eighteenth day, the statue was raised and put onto its platform. Heyerdahl paid the mayor the $100. The mayor also showed Heyerdahl how the statues were probably moved on sleds made of trees. It took many people to pull the sleds. The mayor had learned these things from his father and grandfather. Why hadn't he ever told this to the other scientists who had visited the island? "No one ever asked me," he said.

9   William Mulloy, a member of Heyerdahl's team, stayed on the island to raise more of the statues. From his experiments, he estimated that it would take "thirty men one

[2] **lever** – a long bar that you use to lift or move something by pressing one end

year to carve a stone statue, ninety men two months to move it, and ninety men three months to raise it."

Silent Statues Communicate

10 Although they are silent, these statues communicate to us about the ancient people of Easter Island. To make, move, and raise the statues, these people must have worked hard and cooperated with one another. The statues show us that not only can we learn *about* ancient people, we can also learn *from* them.

After You Read

Comprehension Check

A Read these statements. If a statement is true according to the article, write *T* on the line. If it is false, write *F*.

_____ 1. Easter Island is part of a group of large islands.

_____ 2. People have been living on Easter Island for a long time.

_____ 3. All the statues on the island are completed.

_____ 4. Scientists have been curious about the statues on Easter Island for a long time.

_____ 5. Most of the statues are of young children.

_____ 6. Most of the Easter Islanders know a lot about their past.

_____ 7. The mayor of Easter Island knew how to raise a statue and put it back in its place.

B Write the correct paragraph number to answer each question.

___5___ 1. Which paragraph defines what archaeologists are and tells what they do?

_____ 2. Which paragraph explains how the mayor raised the statue?

_____ 3. Which paragraph asks the questions that the rest of the article will answer?

_____ 4. Which paragraph gives some old explanations about how the statues were built?

_____ 5. Which paragraph tells how the statues were probably moved?

_____ 6. Which paragraph describes what the statues look like?

SKILL FOR SUCCESS

Making Inferences

You have learned that archaeologists **make inferences** about how people lived in the past. They use clues to make their inferences. Readers make inferences, too. Because authors do not always state information directly, good readers need to make inferences while they are reading.

C Check (✔) the statements that are inferences you can make based on the information in the article.

☐ 1. There are no islands near Easter Island.

☐ 2. Early Easter Islanders did not use sophisticated tools.

☐ 3. Volcanic rock is a suitable material for carving things.

☐ 4. It always takes eighteen days to raise a statue.

☐ 5. The statues on Easter Island are different sizes.

☐ 6. Easter Islanders still make huge stone statues today.

☐ 7. Levers are good tools for lifting heavy things.

☐ 8. There is nothing to learn from the people who made the statues of Easter Island.

☐ 9. The people on Easter Island have magical powers.

☐ 10. William Mulloy knew Thor Heyerdahl.

Vocabulary Practice

A Choose the best definition or synonym for each underlined word or phrase. Then compare answers with a partner.

1. Easter Island is a <u>tiny</u> island in the Pacific Ocean surrounded by 1 million square miles (2.59 million square kilometers) of empty Pacific Ocean.
   a. very big
   (b.) very small
   c. very dangerous

2. Long ago, the people farmed the land with simple tools. But they also made huge and <u>magnificent</u> stone statues that have puzzled scientists and everyone else for more than two centuries.
   a. simple
   b. lucky
   c. impressive

3. Think about how difficult it would be to move a stone statue, and you can understand why so many people were <u>baffled</u>.
   a. angry
   b. depressed
   c. puzzled

4. The tools used to <u>carve</u> the statues from the volcanic rock are still there, too.
   a. protect
   b. cut
   c. paint

5. Long before archaeologists came to study the statues, several <u>disasters</u> killed most of the people on the island.
   a. good things that happened
   b. bad things that happened
   c. things that never happened

6. He couldn't <u>figure out</u> how the people had raised the heavy statues and put them on their platforms. He wanted to find out.
   a. count
   b. build
   c. understand

7. The mayor was a <u>descendant</u> of one of the island's oldest families.
   a. someone related to someone who lived in the past
   b. someone who is curious about old families
   c. someone who is new to a place

8. From his experiments, he <u>estimated</u> that it would take "30 men one year to carve a stone statue, 90 men two months to move it, and 90 men three months to raise it."
   a. praised
   b. guessed
   c. rejected

9. Although they are <u>silent</u>, these statues communicate to us about the ancient people of Easter Island.
   a. huge
   b. quiet
   c. heavy

10. To make, move, and raise the statues, these people must have <u>cooperated</u> with one another.
    a. fought
    b. worked
    c. visited

B Cross out the word or phrase in each group that does not belong.

1. baffle   puzzle   confuse   ~~understand~~

2. huge   small   tiny   little

3. silent   noisy   quiet   soundless

4. tragedy   catastrophe   disaster   success

5. simple   marvelous   grand   magnificent

6. estimate   ignore   approximate   guess

7. cooperate   help   predict   work together

8. figure out   discover   understand   confuse

9. grandchild   heir   descendant   archaeologist

SKILL FOR SUCCESS

Learning Word Parts: The Prefix *co-*
The prefix *co-* means "together, joint, jointly." When *co-* is added to a word, it is often easy to guess the word's meaning. For example, you know that a *pilot* is a person who flies a plane. A *copilot* is a person who is flying a plane with another pilot. In this article, you learned that the word *cooperate* means "work together."

C Match each word with the correct definition.

Word	Definition
_____ 1. coworker	**a.** a person who writes a book with another person
_____ 2. coauthor	**b.** to sign a document with another person
_____ 3. cosign	**c.** referring to the education of male and female students at the same time at the same school
_____ 4. coexist	**d.** a person who works with other people at the same place
_____ 5. coeducational	**e.** to exist at the same time or place or to live peacefully with another person or group of people

D Complete each sentence with the correct word from Exercise C.

1. I hope people of all countries can _____ peacefully.

2. My mother will _____ my loan from the bank.

3. I'm having dinner with my new _____. Her desk is right next to mine at the office.

4. Our daughter goes to a _____ high school.

5. Christine is my _____. We write books together.

Make a Time Capsule

A **time capsule** is a container of objects that represent the present time. It is buried so that people in the future can find it and study the objects. The objects they find will help them make inferences about what life was like in the past.

In a small group, make a list of five things you would put in a time capsule to give future generations clues about what life is like today.

1. _____

2. _____

3. _____

4. _____

5. _____

Share your list with the class. If your box were discovered years from now, what would the objects say about you and the time you lived in?

The Nazca Lines

Before You Read

A Discuss these questions with a partner.

1. Look at the photograph. It was taken from an airplane flying above the Nazca desert in Peru. What do you see?
2. How big do you think the design is?
3. Locate Peru on the map on pages 218–219. Have you ever been to Peru?

SKILL
FOR ✔
SUCCESS

Skimming for the Main Idea

Skimming is a way of reading quickly to look for main ideas. When you skim, you don't read every word carefully or stop to look up words you don't know in a dictionary. To skim a paragraph, read the first few sentences and the last few sentences. Look for key words that give you clues about the topic. To skim a longer passage, read the first and last paragraphs. (The first paragraph often introduces the main idea of the passage, and the last paragraph may sum it up.) Then skim the whole passage by reading the first and last sentence of every paragraph. This will give you an overview of the passage and an idea about how it is organized.

B Skim the article one time. Circle the number of the main idea of the article.

1. the life of mathematician Maria Reiche
2. explanations of the mysterious Nazca lines
3. the future of tourism in Peru

C Learn the meanings of the following words and phrase before you read the article.

on purpose (1)	speculate (7)
shocked (2)	agriculture (7)
sparked (2)	fascinate (8)
theory (2)	

The Nazca Lines

by Suzanne Lord

1 The Nazca desert is in southwestern Peru, in South America. It is 38 miles (61 kilometers) from the Pacific Ocean. When you stand on the ground, the area looks dry and rocky. Occasionally, you see small piles of stones that look like someone had put them there on purpose. But it doesn't look mysterious. The Nazca desert just looks like dry land with little piles of rocks. But when you look at the Nazca desert from an airplane, it looks very different. Looking at it from above, you see lots of straight lines that seem like they were drawn with a ruler. You also see triangles, rectangles, or spirals. Or you might see a picture of a monkey, a spider, a whale, a human hand, or a bird. These pictures look like they were drawn on a huge blackboard. The longest straight line is 9 miles (about 15 kilometers) long. From above, the desert is full of mysteries. Who made these lines and pictures? Why did they do it?

2 Most people did not know about the Nazca lines until after the invention of the airplane. When pilots first spotted the lines in the 1920s, they were shocked. They thought that the Nazca lines looked like old landing fields where aircraft could take off and land. The idea of ancient, secret landing fields sparked all kinds of theories about the lines. Some theories sound like science fiction[1] stories.

3 One theory was that the landing fields were built for "pilots" from the lost island of Atlantis. According to legend, Atlantis was a beautiful and peaceful island that sank in an earthquake. When Atlantis sank, the landing fields were not used any longer. They were just left for people to discover thousands of years later.

4 Another theory said that the landing fields were for UFOs[2] coming from outer space. According to this theory, aliens landed on Earth in prehistoric times. The Nazca lines made it easy for the aliens to know where to land.

[1] **science fiction** – stories about imaginary worlds or imaginary developments in science

5 A German mathematician named Maria Reiche had another theory. In 1946, she began studying the lines mathematically. She believed the Nazca lines were astronomical calendars. The lines show movements of the sun, stars, and planets over many years.

6 These sensational[3] theories brought the Nazca lines to the world's attention. From the 1970s on, people started coming to Nazca to see the "ancient landing fields." Today, there is a real airfield in Nazca for planes bringing tourists to the area.

7 Now scientists have more reasonable ideas about the Nazca lines. They know that humans have lived in the area for about 12,000 years. They speculate that ancient people used the lines and pictures in ceremonies or dances. They might have been trying to get the attention of their gods. Since agriculture was very important in their lives, the Nazca lines could have been a way to ensure a good harvest. Or perhaps they were an irrigation[4] system. Another theory is that the animal drawings represented different family groups, or clans, such as the monkey clan, or the spider clan.

8 We may never know the true answers to questions about the Nazca lines, but their mysteries continue to fascinate people. And they raise more questions than they answer. ■

[2] **UFO** – unidentified flying object, a mysterious object in the sky, sometimes thought to be a space vehicle from another world

[3] **sensational** – very exciting or shocking

[4] **irrigation** – a system of supplying water to land or crops

After You Read

Comprehension Check

A Circle the letter of the correct answer.

1. The Nazca desert looks mysterious _____.
   a. from all directions
   b. only from the ground
   c. from the air
   d. (none of the above)

2. The designs on the Nazca desert look like _____.
   a. geometric shapes
   b. animals
   c. perfectly straight lines
   d. (all of the above)

3. After the Nazca lines were discovered, _____.
   a. people were afraid to visit them
   b. many theories developed
   c. pilots began using them to help land their planes
   d. scientists refused to pay any attention to them

4. Maria Reiche was interested in the _____ of the lines.
   a. mathematical relationships
   b. unusual shapes and designs
   c. religious significance
   d. tourist appeal

5. Today, scientists believe the ancient people used the lines and drawings _____.
   a. for ceremonies and dances
   b. to represent different family groups
   c. to attract the attention of their gods
   d. (all of the above)

✓ Making Inferences

B Check (✔) the inferences you can make based on the information in the article.

☐ 1. Tourists are interested in seeing the Nazca lines.

☐ 2. Scientists have discovered the truth about the meaning of the Nazca lines.

☐ 3. Theories about the Nazca lines are becoming more scientific.

☐ 4. Ancient people probably lived in family groups.

☐ 5. The Nazca lines were once landing strips for UFOs.

☐ 6. Ancient people had some form of religion.

SKILL FOR SUCCESS ✓

Scanning for Information
Sometimes you need to find a specific piece of information in a text quickly. To do this, you use a technique called **scanning**. To scan effectively, you need to focus on looking for only that one piece of information. You usually scan to find a name, a date, a time, a place, or a definition. To scan, move your eyes quickly across the text until you find the information you are looking for and then stop reading. Look for key words (important words or words that are repeated), numbers, and names to help you find the information.

C Scan the article for the answer to each question. Work as quickly as possible.

1. How far is the Nazca desert from the Pacific Ocean? _____38 miles_____
2. When did pilots first spot the Nazca lines? _____
3. When did Maria Reiche begin studying the lines mathematically? _____
4. How long have humans lived in the area? _____
5. What is the length of the longest straight line? _____

Vocabulary Practice

A Match each word or phrase with the correct definition.

Word or Phrase	Definition
_____ 1. on purpose	a. a belief about something that has not yet been proven
_____ 2. shocked	b. to guess why something happened
_____ 3. theory	c. to cause something to start
_____ 4. speculate	d. deliberately; not by accident
_____ 5. agriculture	e. to interest someone greatly
_____ 6. fascinate	f. farming and growing crops
_____ 7. spark	g. very surprised

B Cross out the word in each group that does not belong.

1. theory	idea	fact	belief
2. shocked	surprised	stunned	saddened
3. story	legend	style	myth
4. modern	prehistoric	old	ancient
5. calendar	clan	group	tribe
6. guess	speculate	imagine	know
7. fascinate	bore	interest	attract
8. spark	start	stimulate	stop

 SKILL FOR SUCCESS

Learning Antonyms
A word that means the opposite of another word is called an **antonym**. For example, the antonym of *gradually* is *quickly*. Learning antonyms can increase your vocabulary.

C Read the passage. Find an antonym for each word in the chart that follows. Write the antonyms in the chart.

No one really knows how or why Stonehenge was built. These circles of giant stones were placed in a grassy field in southern England nearly 5,000 years ago. Some people believe that the rocks were used as enormous sundials or star clocks. Others think that people used them for religious purposes.

Today, approximately 1 million people visit Stonehenge each year. Visitors can stand near and look at the giant stones. But since 1978, visitors have been prohibited from walking through or touching the 100-foot- (30-meter-) wide circle of stones. Now two busy roads and several parking lots surround the ancient site. Many people don't like this. They think Stonehenge needs to be protected. But there is controversy over how to protect the site. Archaeologists, conservationists, religious groups, and tourists all have different opinions. A group dedicated to preserving historical sites plans to restore Stonehenge to its natural setting. One road will be removed, and another will be routed through a tunnel under the site. The parking lots will become open fields, and a new visitors' center will be built 2½ miles (4 kilometers) away. So on future trips to Stonehenge, pack your walking shoes or plan on taking a shuttle bus to the site.

Word	Antonym
1. allowed	*prohibited*
2. far	
3. small (*find two antonyms*)	
4. agreement	
5. added	
6. quiet	
7. exactly	

Talk It Over

Discuss these questions as a class.

1. How do you think the Nazca lines were made? Do you believe any of the theories in the article?
2. Do you think places like Stonehenge need to be protected? Why or why not?

Do Some Research

Use the Internet or library to find some interesting information about one of the places or things below. Share the information from your research with your classmates.

Angkor Wat (Cambodia)

Loch Ness Monster (Scotland)

Abominable Snowman (Asia)

Pyramids of Giza (Egypt)

Bermuda Triangle (Atlantic Ocean)

Machu Picchu (Peru)

Taj Mahal (India)

Frozen in Time

Before You Read

A Discuss these questions with a partner.

1. Do you ever wonder what life was like thousands of years ago?
2. A mummy is a well-preserved dead body. What do you think we can learn by studying mummies?
3. Have you ever seen a mummy in a museum?
4. Have you ever heard of Otzi the Iceman? If so, what do you know about him?

✓ **Reading with a Purpose**

B You are going to read about the discovery of a very old ice mummy. Write three questions you hope will be answered in the article.

1. _____
2. _____
3. _____

C Learn the meanings of the following words before you read the article.

sensation (1)   weapons (8)
biologists (2)   evidence (8)
belongings (4)   violence (8)
intrigues (8)

Frozen in Time

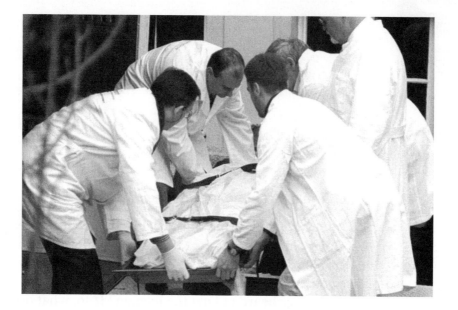

1   One day long ago, a man was climbing in the snow-covered Alps. High up in the mountains, something happened, and he died. Strong winds dried out his body, and soon it was covered with snow. The snow turned into ice, and the man was forgotten. Thousands of years later, in 1991, two tourists found the body in the ice and called the police. The police thought it was the body of someone who had died recently. But when medical examiners inspected it, they realized the body was very old. They didn't realize *how* old until the body was sent to archaeologist Dr. Konrad Spindler at the University of Innsbruck in Austria. When he saw the copper ax found next to the man, Spindler knew that the man had died at least 4,000 years ago. "It may be one of the most important finds in the century!" Spindler exclaimed. Scientists nicknamed the iceman "Otzi" for the Otztaler mountains where he was found. Otzi became an archaeological sensation overnight. Scientists all over the world wanted to study the oldest body ever found in Europe.

Studying the Iceman

2   Since the discovery, scientists have been studying Otzi. To find out exactly when Otzi died, scientists used a special test called carbon dating. The test showed that Otzi died 5,300 years ago. Biologists also tested the body to see if Otzi suffered from any injuries or diseases. They found that he had been very sick three times in the six months before he died. How did they figure that out? By studying one of his fingernails! Scientists used X-rays to look at Otzi's bones. They discovered that several of Otzi's bones had been broken and healed.

3   Scientists were interested in Otzi's diet. They learned what he ate by looking inside his stomach and at his teeth. His teeth were worn down, showing that he ate grains. After studying contents in his stomach, scientists determined that his final meal was meat (probably wild goat and deer) with wheat, plums, and other plants.

4   Otzi lived during a time archaeologists call the Neolithic Age, when people first began to use metal tools and grow food. Otzi was the first Neolithic human ever found with his everyday clothing and belongings. Dr. Markus Egg is an archaeologist with the Romisch-Germanisches Zentral Museum in Mainz, Germany. He and other scientists were very excited about Otzi's clothes. They were the only known examples of Neolithic clothing. "Everything we know about clothing from the Neolithic Age in Europe is from him," Egg said. Otzi was well protected against the cold weather. He was wearing a fur-lined leather coat, leather pants, a cape made of woven grass, a bearskin hat, and leather shoes. His pants and shoes were stuffed with grass for insulation from the cold. The clothes were very sophisticated. "The person who made the clothes initially was obviously skilled," says Egg.

5   Scientists were shocked when they removed Otzi's clothes and found fifty-seven mysterious blue tattoos on his body. They are not sure if the tattoos have a special meaning. But some scientists believe the tattoos were an early type of acupuncture[1]. Before this discovery, it was thought that tattooing did not begin until 2,500 years later.

6   Otzi's other belongings are interesting, too. In addition to the copper ax, Otzi was carrying a knife with a wooden handle, a long bow, feather arrows, and flint[2] for starting fires. Scientists also discovered a beaded necklace that he may have worn for good luck. One of the most important discoveries was a box with two kinds of mushrooms to use as medicine. These mushrooms can fight infections. It seems that Otzi had his own first-aid kit.

Otzi's Mysterious Life and Death

7   Scientists still have many questions about Otzi's life. Where was he from? Why was he so high up in the mountains? Maybe he went there to look for copper. Maybe he was on his way to hunt for animals. Possibly he was on his way to trade with people who lived on the other side of the mountain. No one knows for sure.

8   The mystery of Otzi's death intrigues scientists and the public, too. Every few years, a new theory about how Otzi died makes headlines. At first, scientists believed he had been caught in a blizzard and froze to death alone on the mountain. Another theory was that he died from the diseases he had. Now some people think Otzi died during a fight he had with other people. Scientists discovered the tip of an arrow in his left shoulder. They also detected some cuts on his hands, wrists, and ribs. They have found blood from four other people on his clothes and weapons. This evidence may indicate that Otzi was involved in some kind of violence. Maybe he was killed by enemies. Some mysteries about his life—and his death—may never be solved. ■

---

[1] **acupuncture** – a method used in Chinese medicine in which needles are put into someone's body in order to treat pain or illness

[2] **flint** – a type of very hard black or gray stone

Comprehension Check

A Circle the letter of the correct answer.

1. How did scientists determine the iceman's age?
   a. by using carbon dating
   b. by looking at him
   c. by measuring his height

2. How did scientists find out information about Otzi's diet?
   a. by examining his weapons
   b. by looking inside his stomach and at his teeth
   c. by using carbon dating

3. What is NOT mentioned as a reason Otzi may have been in the mountains?
   a. He went to trade with another group of people.
   b. He was there to look for copper.
   c. He went to look at the beautiful view.

4. Which is evidence that Otzi may have been involved in a fight?
   a. His teeth were worn down.
   b. There was blood from other people on his clothes and weapons.
   c. He was carrying mushrooms that can fight infection.

5. Which is evidence that Otzi ate grains?
   a. His shoes were stuffed with grass.
   b. His teeth were worn down.
   c. He was carrying mushrooms.

✓ **Making Inferences**

B Check (✔) the statements that are inferences based on information in the article.

☐ 1. Otzi knew how to dress to keep warm in the mountains.

☐ 2. Otzi practiced some kind of religion.

☐ 3. Some Neolithic people wore jewelry.

☐ 4. Freezing a body in ice can preserve it for thousands of years.

☐ 5. Otzi had a wife and children.

☐ 6. Otzi was a vegetarian.

7. Otzi came to the mountain to mine copper.

8. People 5,000 years ago knew how to use metal.

9. Scientists can learn about a person's health by studying his or her fingernails.

10. It was very warm the day Otzi died.

11. Some ancient people were skilled at making clothes.

12. Someone shot Otzi with an arrow.

13. The people who lived on the other side of the mountain were Otzi's friends.

14. Some mushrooms can fight infections.

Vocabulary Practice

A Match each word with the correct definition.

Word	Definition
_____ 1. sensation	a. an object used in fighting or war, such as a gun
_____ 2. biologist	b. the things you own, especially those that can be carried
_____ 3. belongings	c. something that causes great excitement or interest
_____ 4. intrigue	d. proof that something is true
_____ 5. weapon	e. someone who studies all forms of life
_____ 6. violence	f. to interest someone a lot, often by being strange or mysterious
_____ 7. evidence	g. actions that hurt people or things

B Circle the letter of the correct answer.

1. Which does a <u>biologist</u> study?
   a. plants and animals   b. tools and machines

2. Which are examples of a person's <u>belongings</u>?
   a. a cell phone and wallet   b. mountains and rivers

3. Which would <u>intrigue</u> you?
   a. a boring movie   b. a mysterious place

4. Which is not a <u>weapon</u>?
   a. a bomb   b. a flag

5. Which would cause a <u>sensation</u>?
   a. the discovery of a new planet   b. the definition of a word

6. Which is an example of <u>violence</u>?
   a. a concert in the park   b. a fight in the street

7. Who looks for <u>evidence</u> at a crime scene?
   a. the police   b. the mailman

SKILL FOR SUCCESS

Using Context Clues

You do not always need to know the exact meaning of an unfamiliar word that you read. Sometimes a general idea of a word is enough to understand the meaning of the sentence or paragraph. One way to guess the meaning of an unfamiliar word is to use **clues from the word's context**—the words and sentences around the word—to guess its meaning. Read the following sentence and guess the meaning of *dashed*:

> When the little boy saw a big spider walking toward him, he became frightened and dashed out of the room.

The context clue is *he became frightened*, so you know that *dashed* probably means "ran quickly."

C Use context clues to choose the definition or synonym for each underlined word. Circle the letter of the answer. Then compare answers with a partner. Do not use a dictionary.

1. The police thought it was the body of someone who had died recently. But when medical examiners <u>inspected</u> it, they realized the body was very old.
   a. looked at closely
   b. ignored completely
   c. threw out carefully

2. After studying contents in his stomach, scientists <u>determined</u> that his final meal was meat (probably wild goat and deer) with wheat, plums, and other plants.
   a. disagreed
   b. found out
   c. planned

3. His pants and shoes were stuffed with grass for <u>insulation</u> from the cold.
   a. examination
   b. protection
   c. discovery

4. Scientists discovered the tip of an arrow in his left shoulder. They also <u>detected</u> some cuts on his hands, wrists, and ribs.
   a. noticed
   b. cleaned
   c. ignored

5. This evidence may indicate that Otzi was involved in some kind of violence. Maybe he was killed by <u>enemies</u>.
   a. people who didn't like him and wanted to hurt him
   b. people who liked him and wanted to help him
   c. people who helped him

SKILL FOR SUCCESS

Learning Word Parts: The Suffixes -ian and -ist
When you add the suffix *-ian* or *-ist* to a word, the new word refers to someone who does something, for example, someone in a certain job or profession. In this chapter, you learned that the word *biologist* means "someone who studies biology."
Note: When *y* is the last letter in a word, drop the *y* before you add *-ian* or *-ist*.

D Complete the chart. Combine the following words with the suffixes in the chart. You may need to use your dictionary.

art   library   music
comedy   magic   violin
economy

Suffix	Job	Clue (a person who . . .)
1. *-ian*	comedian	makes you laugh by acting in a comic (funny) way
2. *-ist*		studies the economy
3. *-ian*		works in a library
4. *-ist*		plays the violin
5. *-ian*		plays music
6. *-ian*		does magic
7. *-ist*		is skilled at creating art

E **Answer each question with the correct word from the chart in Exercise D.**

1. Who would you ask for help finding a book in the library?
   _____

2. Who would you hire to do magic tricks at a party?
   _____

3. Who would you hire to play music at a party? _____
4. Who would know about the trade, industry, or finance of a country?
   _____

5. What kind of entertainer makes you laugh? _____
6. If you wanted to learn how to play the violin, who would you ask to
   teach you? _____
7. What is someone who paints, draws, or makes sculptures called?
   _____

Talk It Over

Discuss these questions as a class.

1. The article refers to Otzi as an "archaeological sensation." In what
   ways was he an archaeological sensation?
2. Why do you think scientists are so interested in the lives of people
   who lived thousands of years ago?
3. It is often said that we study the past to learn more about the present
   and the future. What can we learn about the present and the future
   by studying the past?

Tie It All Together

Discussion

Discuss these questions in a small group.

1. Researchers from many different branches of science are trying to solve the world's mysteries. How do you think that advances in technology will help solve them? What types of technologies will help us solve these unexplained mysteries?
2. The world holds many mysteries from the past. Why do you think we are fascinated by things we cannot fully understand?
3. Do you think there is intelligent life on other planets? Have they visited us on Earth? Do you believe some UFOs are alien spaceships?

Just for Fun

Answer each question by writing the letters of the correct word on the lines provided. Then follow the directions below to solve the word scramble puzzle.

1. When you look at the Nazca plains from above, you might see some perfectly straight
   _l_ _i_ _n_ (_e_) _s_ .
2. What is Mr. Heyerdahl's first name?
   (___) ___ ___ ___
3. Who first spotted the Nazca lines?
   ___ (___) ___ ___ ___ ___
4. The ___ ___ (___) ___ ___ organized the men to move the Easter Island statues.
5. Otzi's body had become a ___ ___ ___ (___) ___ .
6. There are many ___ ___ ___ (___) ___ ___ ___ about the Easter Island statues.
7. What did Otzi have on his body?
   ___ ___ ___ ___ ___ (___)
8. The statues of Easter Island are (___) ___ ___ ___ ___ ___ , but they still communicate to us.
9. Most people didn't know about the Nazca lines until the
   ___ ___ (___) ___ ___ ___ ___ of the airplane.

Now write the nine circled letters below. Then unscramble them to find a word about this unit.

___ ___ ___ ___ ___ ___ ___ ___ ___

10. _____

Easter Island

This video tells the story of a boy who is losing his eyesight and a special visit he makes to Easter Island. Based on the reading in this unit, why do you think he wanted to explore this island?

A Study these words and phrase. Then watch the video.

relics   rub off on
remote   vision

B Read these statements and then watch the video again. If a statement is true, write *T* on the line. If it is false, write *F*.

_____ 1. Easter Island is called Rapanui by the people that live there.

_____ 2. Easter Island is close to the mainland.

_____ 3. No one knows how the statues appeared on the shoreline.

_____ 4. Darren enjoyed climbing near the statues on Easter Island.

_____ 5. Darren and his mother saw a traffic jam during rush hour.

_____ 6. Darren saw two kinds of animals on Easter Island: spiders and horses.

C Discuss these questions with a partner or in a small group.

1. Why are people fascinated by the mysteries of the past? Do they believe there is something magical about Easter Island?
2. Where do you dream of traveling? Why?

Reader's Journal

Think about the topics and ideas you have read about and discussed in this unit. Pick a topic from the list, one of the discussion questions in the unit, or an idea of your own. Write about it for ten to twenty minutes.

• things we can learn from studying the past
• a mysterious place you have visited
• life in the Neolithic Age
• what future generations will think about life now

Vocabulary Self-Test

Complete each sentence with the correct word or phrase.

A biologist   intrigued   speculate
    estimated   sensation

1. We were all _____ by the story she told about her trip to Africa.

2. The police refuse to _____ on the reasons for the crime.

3. We _____ that it would take two hours to drive home, but it took a little longer.

4. Dr. Fenn is a(n) _____ whose area of interest is snakes.

5. News of the discovery in Peru caused a great _____ .

B agriculture   figure out   silent
    fascinate   on purpose   weapon

1. Can you help me? I can't _____ how to do this math problem.

2. _____ is an important part of the country's economy.

3. The police arrested the man for carrying a dangerous _____ .

4. Firefighters believe the fire was started _____ .

5. The crowd became _____ when the president began to speak.

6. The customs of other cultures _____ many people.

C belongings   disaster   theory
    carve   shocked   tiny

1. It is not easy to _____ marble to make a sculpture.

2. Maria Reiche had a _____ that the Nazca lines were astronomical calendars.

3. I left the house in such a hurry that I forgot some of my _____.

4. The earthquake was a terrible _____.

5. Our apartment is _____. It has only two rooms.

6. I was _____ when I saw how much weight she had lost.

D baffled   descendant   magnificent
    cooperated   evidence   sparked

1. Since everyone in the group _____, we got the work done quickly.

2. The police are looking for _____ to solve the crime.

3. The new information _____ a debate among the anthropologists.

4. He said he was a(n) _____ of the first mayor of the city.

5. This is the most _____ sculpture I have ever seen.

6. Even her close friends were _____ by Jane's strange behavior.

MUSIC
TO MY EARS

The poet Henry Wadsworth Longfellow said, "Music is the universal language of mankind." Although music means different things to different people, almost everyone would agree that music is one of life's greatest pleasures. As you read this unit, think about what music means to you.

Points to Ponder

Discuss these questions in a small group.

1. What is your favorite kind of music? What kind of music do you usually listen to?

2. Do you like to sing? Do you like to dance?

3. Do you play an instrument? If so, which one?

4. What kinds of music do people your age listen to in your country? What kind of music do your parents listen to?

5. Do you like to go to concerts? What concerts have you been to recently?

Musicians Who Make a Difference

Before You Read

A Look at the questionnaire about different types of music. Check (✓) the ones you like and dislike. Compare answers with a partner.

Type of Music	Like	Dislike	No Opinion
1. rock			
2. classical			
3. salsa			
4. hip-hop/rap			
5. jazz			
6. rhythm and blues			
7. traditional music (from your country or another country)			
8. reggae			
9. pop			
10. (other) _____			

✓**Using Background Knowledge**

B Look at the photos of the three rock stars in the article. In a small group, discuss what you know about each one.

C Learn the meanings of the following words before you read the article.

charities (2)   humanitarian (3)   solo (4)

causes (2)   overcome (3)   committed (5)

celebrity (3)   victims (3)   accomplished (6)

Musicians Who Make a Difference

Bono

Ricky Martin

Sting

1   Do you recognize the people in the pictures? They are three of the most famous rock stars around. Their names are Bono, Ricky Martin, and Sting. Everyone knows that famous rock stars make a lot of money. But some of them also make a difference, by making the world a better place.

2   Bono, Ricky Martin, and Sting all feel a responsibility to use some of the money they make to help others and to protect the environment. These musicians have all started their own charities to raise money for specific causes.

Bono

3   The Irish rock star Bono is an example of a celebrity musician who is dedicated to humanitarian efforts. Bono originally won international fame with his rock and roll band, U2, which has performed all over the world. Despite his busy recording and touring schedule, Bono makes time to work for causes he believes in. He is especially devoted to helping communities in Africa. Bono has fought hard for many years to overcome problems in Africa, such as AIDS and poverty. He has also helped the victims of the tsunami in Thailand and Hurricane Katrina in New Orleans by organizing charity concerts, celebrity music albums, and other events that raise money.

Ricky Martin

4 Puerto Rican pop idol Ricky Martin has been performing for most of his life. He originally found fame in the youth pop group Menudo and by the age of seventeen was a Latin pop star. He began his solo career in 1990 and quickly gained international fame. Since then, Martin has sold more than 20 million albums.

5 Although Ricky Martin is famous for his music, his work for humanitarian causes has also earned him respect. He gives a large part of his earnings and time to an organization that he started, called the Ricky Martin Foundation. The Ricky Martin Foundation helps children all over the world in important areas such as health care, education, and social justice. Martin is committed to protecting children from being sold into child slavery. Thanks to the efforts of Martin and his foundation, more and more people are becoming aware of the problem of child slavery. The U.S. State Department named Martin as one of its "Heroes in Ending Modern Day Slavery." The department said Martin is "lending a powerful voice to vulnerable[1] children who are unable to speak for themselves" and "reaching tens of millions of people around the world."

Sting

6 Sting is one of the most popular British musicians since the Beatles. His successful career in music started in London nearly thirty years ago with the rock group The Police. Later, Sting became very successful as a solo artist. Sting is also an accomplished songwriter, author, and actor.

7 Many people say, however, that it is his role as a political activist[2] that makes him a superstar. Sting has been a longtime supporter of Amnesty International. This organization helps people around the world who are fighting for human rights[3]. Sting has raised millions of dollars for Amnesty International causes. Sting is also dedicated to protecting the environment, especially the disappearing rainforests of the world. In 1989, Sting and his wife, Trudie Styler, started the Rainforest Foundation. The goal of the foundation is to help protect rainforests from destruction and to support the native people who live there.

8 We should all thank musicians like Bono, Ricky Martin, and Sting who are dealing with important issues that affect the world today. When it comes to raising money for humanitarian causes, popular musicians get the message out loud and clear. ■

[1] **vulnerable** – easily hurt or attacked

[2] **political activist** – someone who works to make changes in the government

[3] **human rights** – basic rights and freedom that every person deserves, such as fair and equal treatment

After You Read

Comprehension Check

Complete the chart with information from the article.

	Birthplace	**Band**	**Causes/Foundations**
Bono	*Ireland*		
Ricky Martin			
Sting			

Vocabulary Practice

F Y I

If the track of a CD (compact disc) were laid out in a straight line, instead of a circle, it would be 8 miles (13 kilometers) long.

A Match each word with the correct definition.

Word

_____ 1. charity

_____ 2. overcome

_____ 3. victim

_____ 4. humanitarian

_____ 5. solo

_____ 6. celebrity

_____ 7. causes

_____ 8. committed

_____ 9. accomplished

Definition

a. someone who has been hurt or killed or affected by a bad situation

b. a famous person

c. an organization that gives money or gifts to people who need help

d. things you believe in and fight for

e. concerned with improving the lives of other people

f. working or performing alone; not part of a group

g. to succeed in controlling a problem

h. talented

i. dedicated

B Complete each sentence with the correct word.

charity   committed   solo

1. I gave money to the Save the Trees Foundation. It is my favorite _____.

2. Paulo is a _____ artist. He always sings alone.

3. Ricky Martin is _____ to helping children around the world.

cause   humanitarian   victims

4. Fighting for human rights for all people is an important

_____.

5. Albert Einstein was the most famous scientist of his time. He also cared deeply for the welfare of others and was a great

_____.

6. Many of the _____ of the hurricane lost their homes.

accomplished   celebrity   overcome

7. Bono is a(n) _____ musician.

8. They have worked hard to _____ their problems.

9. He was already an international _____ by the time he was twenty.

SKILL FOR SUCCESS ✓

Learning Idioms: Expressions with _Make_

An **idiom** is a group of words that has a special meaning. The meaning of the group of words as a whole is different from the meanings of the individual words. For example, in this chapter, you saw idioms with the word _make: make a difference, make money,_ and _make time._ Learning idioms is an important part of learning a new language and will help you become a more fluent reader.

C **Complete each conversation with the expressions from the list above it. Use each expression only once.**

1. make an exception   making money   make ends meet
   A: John got fired from his job last month.

   B: I know. Now he isn't _____, and he's having

                                           a.

   a hard time trying to _____.

                                           b.

   A: If he doesn't pay his rent by June 1, he is going to have to move out of his apartment.

   B: Maybe the landlord will _____ and let him

                                           c.

   pay the rent a few weeks late.

   A: I hope so.

2. make a good impression   make up your mind
   A: I'm nervous about my job interview. I don't know what to wear. I

   want to _____.

                               a.

   B: Why don't you wear your new black suit? It looks good on you.

A: I was thinking of that, but I really like my blue one better.

B: Well, you'd better _____ and get dressed.
b.
Your interview is in an hour.

3. make a difference   make time   make excuses

A: Our organization is planting some new trees in the park on Saturday. Can you help us?

B: I'm sorry. I'm too busy this weekend. I don't have time.

A: Don't _____! It's for a good cause, and it
a.
will _____ in our community.
b.

B: OK. I guess I can _____ to help out. I'll just
c.
have to rearrange my schedule.

Talk It Over   Discuss these questions as a class.

1. How important is music in your life? What role does it play in your life?
2. How can music help people from different cultures understand one another better?
3. Do you buy or listen to music in English? Is it always important to you to understand the lyrics?

Make a CD   Work with a partner to make a list of ten songs you would record onto a CD. Complete the chart. Share your list with the rest of the class.

Track	Song	Artist
1		
2		
3		
4		
5		
6		
7		
8		
9		
10		

Happy Birthday to a Musical Genius

Before You Read

A Talk to your classmates to learn about their musical interests.

Find someone in your class who . . .	Name of Student	Information
has been to a concert recently.		What concert?
plays a musical instrument.		What instrument?
listens to classical music.		How often?
owns one or more Mozart CDs.		How many?

✓ **Skimming for the Main Idea**

B Skim the article one time. Then circle the statement you think describes the main idea.

1. Mozart lived a short life, but he wrote many compositions.
2. People in cities all over the world celebrated Mozart's birthday.
3. Mozart's birthday celebration began in Sydney, Australia.

C Learn the meanings of the following words and phrase before you read the article.

genius (1)   kick off (3)
composers (2)   praised (5)
masterpieces (2)   renovated (6)
delighted (3)

HAPPY BIRTHDAY TO A MUSICAL GENIUS

The World Celebrates the 250th Birthday of Wolfgang Amadeus Mozart

by Dina El Nabli

1 From Salzburg, Austria, to Sydney, Australia, people all over the world listened to the music of Wolfgang Amadeus Mozart on January 27, 2006. They were celebrating the 250th birthday of a musical genius. With his music as the soundtrack, people celebrated Mozart's life and work at concerts, opera performances, festivals, museum exhibits, discussions, and more.

Remembering a Musical Genius

2 Mozart is one of the greatest and most beloved composers in history. He was born on a snowy night on January 27, 1756. Mozart's father, Leopold, was a violinist and composer. By the time Mozart was three, he was playing on a keyboard. By age five, he had written his first composition. During his short life, Mozart composed about 630 works, including 41 symphonies and 27 piano concertos. Many were masterpieces that continue to be studied by piano students everywhere. He died at the age of thirty-five.

Starting the Party in Sydney

3 The worldwide celebration of Mozart's life began in Sydney, Australia, where the Sydney Symphony Orchestra performed Mozart's music. "We were delighted that it fell to Sydney Symphony to kick off the world's first Mozart birthday celebration," said Libby Christie, managing director of the Sydney Symphony Orchestra. Other celebrations were held in Beijing, China; Tokyo, Japan; Berlin, Germany; Paris, France; London, England; Vienna, Austria; New York City, U.S.A.; and many other cities around the world.

Celebrating in Austria

4 Many of the events took place in Mozart's native country, Austria, and especially in Salzburg, his birthplace, and Vienna, where he died. Both Austrian cities offered visitors tours of places Mozart visited, including his

favorite restaurants and the homes of his friends and enemies.

5 In Salzburg, stores were filled with everything from Mozart chocolates to Mozart umbrellas. In addition to books about Mozart's life and CDs of his music, Mozart fans bought Mozart toys, T-shirts, baseball caps, and even golf balls. Posters that read "Happy Birthday, Mozart" hung throughout the city. There was a big street party with a huge birthday cake weighing more than 300 pounds (136 kilograms). Celebrations in Mozart's hometown continued throughout the year. Over the summer, 22 of Mozart's works were presented at the Festival of Salzburg. Salzburg Governor, Gabi Burgstaller, praised Mozart for making Salzburg the city it is today. "Mozart would have existed without Salzburg, but Salzburg, this Salzburg, would not exist without Mozart," Burgstaller said.

6 In Vienna, where Mozart spent the last ten years of his life, only one of his homes still exists today. It was renovated for a total cost of about $9.8 million and was renamed Mozart House. It was in this house that Mozart composed *The Marriage of Figaro*. This opera is one of the most beautiful pieces of music ever written. It was also in this house that Mozart taught the sixteen-year-old Beethoven. Although the renovation was expensive, it was well worth the money and effort. Mozart House was opened to the public on January 27, 2006, and visitors can tour exhibitions dedicated to his life and works. Visiting Mozart House is truly a memorable experience and a wonderful way to celebrate his birthday.

After You Read

Comprehension Check

A Read these statements. If a statement is true according to the article, write *T* on the line. If it is false, write *F*.

_____ 1. Mozart was the first person in his family to compose music.

_____ 2. Piano students today still study and play the works of Mozart.

_____ 3. Mozart composed *The Marriage of Figaro* in Salzburg.

_____ 4. Celebrations honoring Mozart's birthday were held all over the world.

_____ 5. Mozart was very old when he died.

_____ 6. Mozart composed more than 600 works.

SKILL FOR SUCCESS ✓

Identifying Facts and Opinions
Facts are statements that can be proven to be true. **Opinions** are statements that describe someone's feelings or beliefs about a topic. The ability to distinguish between facts and opinions will help you to make judgments about what you read.

B Decide if each statement is a fact or an opinion. Check (✓) the correct box.

	Fact	Opinion
1. Mozart is one of the greatest and most beloved composers in history.		
2. During his short life, he composed about 630 works, including 41 symphonies and 27 piano concertos.		
3. This opera is one of the most beautiful pieces of music ever written.		
4. "Mozart would have existed without Salzburg, but Salzburg, this Salzburg, would not exist without Mozart."		
5. The house was renovated for a total cost of about $9.8 million.		
6. Although the renovation was expensive, it was well worth the money and effort.		
7. Mozart spent the last ten years of his life in Vienna.		
8. It was in this house that Mozart composed *The Marriage of Figaro*.		

Vocabulary Practice

A Match each word or phrase with the correct definition.

Word or Phrase	Definition
_____ **1.** genius	**a.** pleased
_____ **2.** composer	**b.** repaired or improved a building, etc.
_____ **3.** masterpiece	**c.** to start something
_____ **4.** kick off	**d.** great talent or intelligence
_____ **5.** praise	**e.** someone who writes music
_____ **6.** renovated	**f.** an excellent piece of music, art, etc.
_____ **7.** delighted	**g.** to express approval

B Complete each sentence with the correct word or phrase from Exercise A.

composer	genius	masterpieces	renovated
delighted	kick off	praises	

1. Let's _____ the celebration with a parade.

2. Mozart is a famous _____ who wrote many _____.

3. The mayor's house was _____ last year.

4. Mozart's musical _____ is recognized around the world.

5. Our orchestra is _____ to present *The Marriage of Figaro* tonight.

6. The piano teacher _____ her students when they play well.

SKILL FOR SUCCESS

Learning Compound Words
A compound word is a combination of two or more words. For example, *birthplace* is a compound word. It is made of the two words *birth* and *place*. If you know the meanings of these two words, you can guess what *birthplace* means. In this chapter, you read several compound words: *masterpiece, worldwide, keyboard, hometown, birthplace.*

C Complete each sentence with the correct compound word. Use your dictionary to help you.

birthrate	keyhole
blackboard	mastermind
citywide	nationwide
homesick	skateboard
homework	workplace

1. I've been living in the United States for six months. I miss my family and friends. I'm really _____.

2. We need to be careful about fire safety in the _____. We have fire alarms in every office.

3. I can't open the door. My key got stuck in the _____.

4. You should wear a helmet when you ride on your _____.

5. He planned the whole robbery. He was the _____ of the crime.

6. We have stores all over the country. It is a _____ chain of stores.

7. The teacher will write the words on the _____.

8. I have to do twenty math problems, write an English essay, and read fifty pages in my history book. As you can see, I have a lot of _____.

9. The number of babies born every year keeps growing. The _____ is increasing.

10. Everyone in the city must pay sales tax. It's a _____ tax.

Choose the Winners

You are organizing a music awards event for music in your country. Write your choice for the winner of each category in the chart. Then find a partner and write his or her choices in the chart.

	Your Choice	Your Partner's Choice
Best Female Solo Artist		
Best Male Solo Artist		
Best Single of the Year		
Best Album of the Year		
Best Music Video of the Year		
Best New Musician		

The Power of Music

Before You Read

A Discuss these questions in a small group.

1. Do you like to listen to music when you work or study? Why or why not?
2. Have you ever noticed that some music relaxes you? What kind of music relaxes you?
3. Does music ever give you energy? If so, what kind of music gives you energy?
4. Have you ever noticed the background music played in elevators, offices, stores, and restaurants? Check (✓) the adjectives you would use to describe background music. Then compare your list with those of your classmates.

☐ 1. pleasant
☐ 2. energetic
☐ 3. boring
☐ 4. relaxing
☐ 5. irritating
☐ 6. (other) _____

✓ **Previewing and Predicting**

B Preview the article by looking at the title, subtitle, headings, words in italics, and cartoon. Then make predictions by checking (✓) the topics you think will be discussed.

☐ 1. the effect of music on shoppers
☐ 2. an explanation of what background music is
☐ 3. how Muzak affects workers
☐ 4. what to order at a restaurant

C The following words all appear in the article. Make sure you know the meanings before you read it.

patient (3)   annoying (7)

lively (3)   calming (7)

clients (6)   inspirational (7)

essential (6)

The Power of Music

1   Every day more than 100 million people hear the sound of background music. They hear it while they are working in offices, shopping in stores, and eating in restaurants. They even hear it while they are sitting in the dentist's chair. Why is background music played in so many places? The answer is easy. Music is such a powerful force that it can affect people's behavior.

Music Affects Shoppers, Diners, and Employees

2   Studies show that background music can affect the sales of a business. Ronald Milliman, a marketing[1] professor, measured the effects that fast music, slow music, and no music had on customers in a supermarket. He found that fast music did not affect sales very much when compared with no music. However, slow music made a big difference. Listening to music played slowly made shoppers move more slowly. When slow music was played, shoppers bought more and sales increased 38 percent.

3   Milliman also found that restaurant owners can use music to their advantage. In the evening, playing slow music lengthens the amount of time customers spend in the restaurant. It also makes customers who are waiting for a table more patient. At lunchtime, restaurants want people to eat more quickly so they can serve more customers. Playing lively music at lunch encourages customers to eat quickly and leave.

4   Many businesses play background music to improve their workers' performance and moods. Research shows that workers often feel less stressed, bored, and tired when they listen to music. Music can also give them energy when they need it. All of these things help make them more productive.

[1] **marketing** – business activities (such as advertising) that persuade customers to buy a product

Selling Background Music

5   The most popular supplier of background music is a company called Muzak, which supplies 60 percent of the commercial background music in the United States. With offices around the world, Muzak serves more than 400,000 businesses in fifteen different countries including Japan, Canada, Mexico, and the Netherlands. Today, Muzak officials estimate that 100 million people hear Muzak tunes every day. That's a lot of music for one company!

6   Unlike other kinds of music, Muzak's primary purpose is not to entertain listeners. Bob Finigan is the marketing director for Muzak. He believes, "Every business has a certain look, feel, and personality that can be expressed through music." Muzak tries to capture that look, feel, and personality through its music. People called *audio architects* carefully design the Muzak programs. The audio architects choose the songs from Muzak's huge collection of more than 2 million songs. The songs represent many different types of music including jazz, rock, and pop. Chris McLain, a Muzak account executive in Gainesville, Florida, explains why music plays such an important role in business. "Every business wants to create an experience for its customers and employees. Nothing creates that experience more powerfully than music," he says. He tells his clients that the right music is essential to creating an experience that everyone will remember. If that is accomplished, Muzak has met its goal.

Mixed Opinions about Muzak

7   What do people really feel about the background music that invades our daily lives? Becky Branford, a reporter for BBC News Website, asked some people in a busy hotel district in London what they thought about Muzak. Many of the people she talked to said they found Muzak annoying and boring. However, other people said Muzak is enjoyable and has a calming effect. Here are some samples of what people said:

- "It depends on the music," said Sue, a tourist from Los Angeles. "If it's elevator music, it annoys me. But if people take the trouble to make the music interesting, it can be nice."
- Ray, a businessman from Northern Ireland, said he found it "tiresome." "Unless it's music I like, I don't really want to hear it. Inspirational music, I find, does lift my spirits."
- Tracy, who worked at one of the hotels, had this to say: "I find it quite irritating actually, although some of the classical music's quite nice—I do enjoy that."
- Abiyadou, a businessman from Nigeria, was more enthusiastic. "It's good, it's very good. Very nice. The classical music is not too loud—it's nice and gentle. Yes, it definitely relaxes me," he said.

8   Whether you like to listen to background music or not, most people agree that it is powerful. It has the capability of changing our moods and evoking strong reactions both for and against. How about you? What do you think of Muzak? ■

Comprehension Check

A Circle the correct answer.

1. If a restaurant owner wants to get customers in and out quickly during lunch, what kind of music should he or she play?
   a. fast music
   b. slow music
   c. no music

2. According to the article, who does Muzak affect?
   a. workers
   b. customers
   c. workers and customers

3. Who is Ronald Milliman?
   a. an employee of Muzak
   b. a customer at a supermarket
   c. a marketing professor

4. What is the main purpose of Muzak?
   a. to entertain the public
   b. to increase productivity
   c. to put people to sleep

5. Which is not true of Muzak soundtracks?
   a. They are carefully designed.
   b. They include many types of music.
   c. They are speeded up so shoppers will buy more.

6. Which is true about people who listen to Muzak?
   a. Everyone likes it.
   b. No one likes it.
   c. Some people like it.

7. Which statement expresses something Muzak officials believe?
   a. The right music creates a positive experience for customers and employees.
   b. Customers won't remember the music they hear in a store.
   c. A store's image is not related to music.

8. Why does the author report what people said about Muzak?
   a. to show that almost everyone likes Muzak
   b. to prove that very few people notice Muzak
   c. to show that people have different opinions about Muzak

✓ Identifying Facts and Opinions

B The author states both facts and opinions in the article. Make a list of three of the facts from the article and three of the author's opinions. Compare answers with a partner.

Facts

1. _____

2. _____

3. _____

Opinions

1. _____

2. _____

3. _____

✓ Identifying the Main Idea of a Paragraph

C Circle the answer to each question about the main ideas of the paragraphs in the article.

1. What is the main idea of paragraph 1?
   a. Muzak is played in offices, stores, and restaurants.
   b. Muzak is played to influence people's behavior.
   c. People hear Muzak on elevators and on phones.

2. Which statement best expresses the main idea of paragraph 2?
   a. Ronald Milliman is a marketing professor.
   b. When slow music was played, sales increased 38 percent.
   c. Background music can help or hurt a store's sales.

3. What is the main idea of paragraph 3?
   a. Restaurants can use background music to influence customers.
   b. People want to eat quickly at lunch.
   c. Slow music encourages customers to spend more time eating.

4. What is the main idea of paragraph 5?
   a. About 100 million people hear Muzak tunes every day.
   b. Muzak has offices around the world.
   c. Muzak is the most popular supplier of background music.

5. What is the main idea of paragraph 6?
   a. Audio architects carefully design the Muzak programs.
   b. Muzak's primary goal is to capture the look, feel, and personality of a business.
   c. Bob Finigan is the marketing director for Muzak.

Vocabulary Practice

A Circle the letter of the correct answer.

1. A <u>lively</u> person has _____.
   a. a lot of energy   b. very little energy

2. If you think a piece of music was <u>inspirational</u>, it _____.
   a. made you want to do something   b. put you to sleep

3. Which are <u>essential</u> for most plants to grow?
   a. water and sun   b. money and information

4. A good business _____ its <u>clients</u>.
   a. ignores   b. pays attention to

5. A <u>patient</u> person _____.
   a. doesn't mind waiting   b. hates to wait for anything

6. If you play <u>calming</u> music for a baby, it will probably _____ the baby.
   a. wake   b. relax

7. Which sound do you find <u>annoying</u>?
   a. the honking of a car's horn   b. soft background music

B Cross out the word in each group that does not belong.

1. lively	active	slow	enthusiastic
2. necessary	essential	important	extra
3. client	seller	customer	buyer
4. patient	angry	annoyed	nervous
5. annoying	irritating	pleasing	bothersome
6. calming	annoying	relaxing	soothing
7. hopeful	stimulating	boring	inspirational

✓**Learning Synonyms**

C Read the paragraph. Find a synonym for each word or phrase in the chart that follows. Write the synonyms in the chart.

A new study suggests that the type of music you listen to while you eat influences both the amount of food you eat and the length of time it takes you to eat. Researchers at the Johns Hopkins Medical Institutions served three meals to ninety people. The first meal was served without music. One-third of the diners asked for second helpings, and the meal took about forty minutes to finish. Three weeks later, the researchers served the same people the same food while playing lively tunes. This time, half of the diners asked for second helpings, and they finished eating in only thirty-one minutes. The final meal was served with slow, relaxing music. Many diners did not finish their first helpings, and only a few people requested seconds. It also took them nearly an hour to finish their meal. This time, the diners said that they felt fuller and more satisfied than they did after the previous meals, even though they actually ate less. Some participants even claimed the meal tasted better.

Word or Phrase	Synonym
1. asked for	
2. almost	
3. complete	
4. songs	
5. upbeat	
6. said	
7. calming	
8. earlier	

Talk It Over

Discuss these questions as a class.

1. How do you feel about the use of music to change people's behavior?
2. According to author Otto Friedrich, "Muzak seems to inspire great passion for or against." Which side are you on?
3. The musician Philip Glass said, "The range (of music) is enormous—opera at the top and Muzak at the bottom." Do you agree with him?

UNIT 3 Tie It All Together

Discussion

Discuss these questions in a small group.

1. How have computers and the Internet changed the way people enjoy music?
2. Besides entertainment, what are some other benefits of music?
3. Beate Gordon, a Russian who grew up in Japan and then lived in the United States, said, "Although music is often said to be a 'universal language,' listening to music based on ideas we are not used to and played on instruments we have not heard before can be like tasting a new food. We may approach it warily, almost sure we won't like it because we have not tried it." Do you agree with Gordon's opinion?
4. Thousands of years ago, the Chinese philosopher Confucius said, "Music produces a kind of pleasure which human nature cannot do without." Do you agree with him?

Just for Fun

Solve the puzzle. Use the clues to answer the questions that follow.

John, Carol, Steve, Tom, Mary, and David all like music. Two of the people are teachers, and the other four are students. Each teacher gives lessons in two of the following instruments: tuba, saxophone, guitar, or drums. Each student takes lessons in one of those instruments.

CLUES
- The drum student is not a woman.
- Carol has never played a brass instrument*.
- Mary has never met Tom.
- Steve often helps the saxophone teacher give lessons.
- The tuba teacher told her student to practice more.
- John is the saxophone student.
- Steve is a teacher.

1. Who are the teachers? _____ _____
2. Which two instruments do they each teach?
   Teacher 1: _____ _____
   Teacher 2: _____ _____
3. Who are the students? _____ _____ _____
   _____
4. Which instrument is each one learning? _____ _____
   _____ _____

* **brass instrument** – a wind instrument made of metal, such as a trumpet or tuba

Wynton Marsalis

In this video, you will hear about a new jazz concert theater in New York City. Wynton Marsalis, one of the most famous jazz musicians in the world today, is the driving force behind the House of Swing, the new home of Marsalis's band, "Jazz at Lincoln Center." Why do you think Marsalis wanted to create this performance space? What do you think his goals might be?

A Study these words and phrases. Then watch the video.

ascendance	consciousness	sought after
committed	diversity	venue
congregate	humble	

B Read the list of events. Watch the video again and put the events in chronological order (1–5).

_____ Jazz was born in New Orleans.

_____ Marsalis won the Grammy Award for both jazz and classical music in the same year.

_____ A concert theater, the House of Swing, opened in New York City.

_____ Marsalis won the Pulitzer Prize for Music.

_____ Marsalis joined the Jazz Messengers.

C Discuss these questions with a partner or in a small group.

1. In the video, Wynton Marsalis says that music brings people together. Do you agree with him? Give examples.
2. Have you ever been to a jazz performance? If so, describe the experience.
3. Do you think the large performance hall that Marsalis has helped to design will be a success? Why or why not?

Reader's Journal

Think about the topics and ideas you have read about and discussed in this unit. Pick a topic from the list, one of the discussion questions in the unit, or an idea of your own. Write about it for ten to twenty minutes.

- your favorite kind of music
- your favorite musician or band
- the traditional music of your country

Vocabulary Self-Test

Complete each sentence with the correct word or phrase.

A
| accomplished | client | kick off | renovate |
| celebrity | inspirational | lively | solo |

1. The children in my class this year have a lot of energy. I am so glad they are a(n) _____ group.

2. Let's meet at 4:00. I have a lunch date with an important _____.

3. The graduation speaker talked about the importance of hard work. His speech was quite _____.

4. When the Beatles broke up, Paul McCartney began a(n) _____ career.

5. Today's game will _____ at 3:00.

6. It cost the Chungs a lot of money to _____ their house.

7. Diego Rivera was a(n) _____ artist. His paintings hang in many museums.

8. I don't think it would be fun to be a(n) _____. They have no privacy.

B
| charities | essential | overcome | praised |
| composers | genius | patient | |

1. It is important for teachers to be _____ with their students.

2. Beethoven was one of the greatest _____ in the world.

3. Mr. Perreira _____ Elmir for the high quality of his work.

4. Several _____ sent aid to those who lost their homes in the earthquake.

5. Ali is really good with words. He is a(n) _____ at crossword puzzles.

6. Good food is _____ for good health.

7. I'm trying to _____ my fear of heights.

C
annoying	cause	delighted	masterpiece
calming	committed	humanitarian	victims

1. I don't mind giving money if it is for a good _____.

2. Several of the _____ of the fire are still in the hospital.

3. Tracy has the _____ habit of leaving her dirty dishes all over the apartment.

4. The Red Cross is concerned with getting _____ aid to those who need it.

5. We are _____ that you can come to our wedding.

6. Leonardo da Vinci is probably best known for his _____ the *Mona Lisa*.

7. Maria has a soft voice. We've noticed that she has a(n) _____ effect on the kids.

8. Ms. Alynn works hard. She is a very _____ teacher.

GETTING DOWN TO BUSINESS

Whether you are buying a bus ticket, a new pair of shoes, or a multimillion-dollar company, buying and selling are an important part of life. In this unit, you will read about the ways business affects us all.

Points to Ponder

Think about these questions and discuss them in a small group.

1. Where do you think the scene in the cartoon is taking place? Did the cartoon make you laugh? If so, why is it funny?

2. You have learned that playing music in stores can increase sales. What else can you think of that companies could do to increase sales?

3. Oil is an expensive source of energy. What other kinds of energy could we use that are less expensive?

The Big Business of Fads

Before You Read

A Discuss these questions with a partner.

1. A product that is very popular for a short time is called a *fad*. Why do you think things become fads?
2. What are some of the fads that are popular today?
3. Look at the photos below and in the article. Do you recognize any of these fads that were popular at different times?

B Learn the meanings of the following words and phrases before you read the article.

catches on (1)   mood (5)
practical (2)   made a mint (6)
invested (2)   tips (6)
sold like hotcakes (4)   word of mouth (7)

The Big Business of Fads

1 Once in a while, someone has a great idea that becomes a fad, a product that is very popular for a short time. Some fads are lasting; others just disappear. If a fad really catches on, the creator can become rich. Below are the stories of some fads that caught on and made their creators millionaires.

Silly Putty

2 Silly Putty was one of the most popular toys of the twentieth century. Scientists at General Electric  discovered it by accident in 1944. They were doing experiments when they discovered a material like rubber that could do many things. It could bounce like a ball, stretch like chewing gum, and even copy cartoons in the newspaper. The scientists at General Electric couldn't think of any practical uses for it. But in 1949, one of the scientists, Peter Hodgson, decided it would make a great toy. He called it Silly Putty. Hodgson invested $150 in his idea. He sold small bags of the putty in plastic eggs. It was an instant success. Millions of eggs of Silly Putty have been sold and continue to sell to this day.

The Slinky

3 Richard James invented the Slinky in 1945 when he was twenty-six years old. This invention was  also an accident. James was working as an engineer. He was trying to make a spring to use on boats at sea. The spring he developed didn't work for that purpose, but it did make a great toy for kids. Richard and his wife, Betty, began to manufacture and sell Slinkies. A Slinky was just a long piece of flat wire coiled[1] into circles, but it could do lots of things. The Slinky could, for example, "walk" down stairs. It could open and close like an accordion[2]. It soon became a favorite toy of the 1950s, and it is still popular today.

The Hula Hoop

4 Arthur Melin and Richard Knerr became rich selling Hula Hoops, but they didn't invent them. They borrowed an idea from Australia, where students were using wooden hoops to

---

[1] **coiled** – twisted into circles

[2] **accordion** – a musical instrument that you pull in and out while pushing buttons to produce different notes

exercise. Melin and Knerr decided to make similar hoops out of plastic. They called their hoops Hula Hoops. In 1958, Melin and Knerr started manufacturing the hoops in lots of bright colors. Hula Hoops sold like hotcakes and became one of the biggest fads of all time. Melin and Knerr sold 25 million Hula Hoops in two months. Almost 100 million international orders soon followed.

The Mood Ring

5   Joshua Reynolds, a thirty-three-year-old New Yorker, created and marketed the original Mood  Ring in 1975. The rings became popular very quickly, and soon thousands of people were wearing Mood Rings. Here's how they work: The ring reacted to changes in your body temperature which made the stone in the ring change colors. The colors supposedly showed your mood at the moment. Warm body temperatures produced bright colors like blue or green. This meant you were in a bright or happy mood. Colder body temperatures produced dark colors like black or brown. These colors meant you were depressed, or in a dark mood.

The Pet Rock

6   Gary Dahl, of Los Gatos, California, made a mint selling Pet Rocks. He came up  with the idea while joking with friends about his easy-to-care-for pet, a rock. This pet ate nothing and didn't bark or chew the furniture. Pet Rocks were just a rock sold with a funny user's guide that included tips on how to handle an excited rock and how to teach it tricks. The fad caught on immediately. More than a million people bought Pet Rocks as Christmas gifts in 1975. By 1976, Gary Dahl was a millionaire, and Pet Rocks were the nation's favorite pets.

The Beanie Baby

7   Toymaker Ty Warner was the creator of the amazingly successful 1990s toy, Beanie Babies. Warner wanted to produce soft stuffed animals that were small enough to fit in a child's hand and  cost about five dollars. His idea worked. The first Beanie Babies were produced in 1993. Warner didn't have to advertise Beanie Babies; their popularity spread by word of mouth. By the 1995 holiday season, they were a nationwide fad, and people began collecting them. By 1996, Beanie Babies were everywhere, and Warner was a rich man. Today the fad has died, but collectors, both adults and children, continue to buy, sell, and trade Beanie Babies.

8   As you can see, over the years, many fads have come and gone. However, you can be certain that a new fad will come along soon and that someone will make a fortune on it. ∎

After You Read

Comprehension Check

A Circle the letter of the correct answer.

1. Which fad was NOT invented by accident?
   a. the Slinky
   b. the Beanie Baby
   c. Silly Putty

2. Which statement is TRUE about fads?
   a. All fads make their creators rich and famous.
   b. Some fads are popular for a long time; others disappear quickly.
   c. Only scientists can invent something that becomes a fad.

3. Which fad was borrowed from an idea in Australia?
   a. Silly Putty
   b. the Mood Ring
   c. the Hula Hoop

4. Who did not advertise his product?
   a. Gary Dahl
   b. Ty Warner
   c. Richard James

B Read these statements. If a statement is true according to the article, write *T* on the line. If it is false, write *F*.

_____ 1. The colors of Mood Ring stones changed as the wearer's body temperature changed.

_____ 2. Slinkies and Silly Putty were popular at the same time.

_____ 3. Pet Rocks were sold with a user's guide because they were hard to care for.

_____ 4. Beanie Babies are still bought, sold, and traded today.

_____ 5. Hula Hoops took a long time to catch on.

_____ 6. People do not buy Silly Putty anymore.

SKILL FOR SUCCESS ✔

Using Graphic Organizers: Charts
Graphic organizers are a visual representation of information. They help you understand, organize, and remember information from a reading. A **chart** is one kind of graphic organizer.

C Complete the chart with information from the article.

Fad	Creator	Date	Description
the Hula Hoop			
	Ty Warner		
			a rubber-like material that can bounce and stretch
the Slinky			
the Mood Ring			
		1975	

Vocabulary Practice

A Match each word or phrase with the correct definition.

Word or Phrase

_____ 1. practical

_____ 2. invest

_____ 3. mood

_____ 4. tip

_____ 5. catch on

_____ 6. word of mouth

_____ 7. sell like hotcakes

_____ 8. make a mint

Definition

a. to spend money in order to make a profit later

b. a helpful piece of advice

c. the way you feel at a specific time

d. sensible

e. to sell a lot of something quickly

f. to become popular

g. to make a lot of money

h. passing information by talking about it

B Complete each sentence with the correct word or phrase.

catches on   mood   tips
invested   practical   word of mouth
make a mint   sold like hotcakes

1. Tickets to the concert _____. There are none left.

2. I _____ $500 in my brother's new business.

3. The company didn't advertise the job. I heard about it by _____.

82   UNIT 4

4. This book has lots of _____ advice about how to start a new business.

5. I am opening a jewelry store on West Charles Street. I hope it will be very successful and I will _____.

6. Marlie gave us several _____ on good restaurants in Rio before we left on our trip.

7. Our teacher was very happy today. He was in a really good _____.

8. If a fad _____, the creator can make a lot of money.

SKILL FOR SUCCESS

Learning Idioms: Expressions about Money and Business
English has many idioms that have to do with money and business. For example, in this chapter, you learned the idiom *sell like hotcakes*.

C Work with a partner. Study these idioms about money and business.

1. *To get down to business* means "to get serious about working on something important."
2. *Money talks* is used to say that people who have money can usually get whatever they want.
3. *To pay through the nose* means "to pay much too much money for something."
4. *To be broke* means "to have no money."
5. *Mind your own business* is used to tell someone not to ask questions or show too much interest in other people's lives.

Now, with your partner, create a situation in which you would use each of the idioms.

1. <u>You and your roommate have had a great first semester at your new school. You've met a lot of interesting people and had a lot of fun. Final exams start next week, and you realize you are really going to have to get down to business if you want to pass your courses.</u>

2. _____

_____

_____

_____

3. _____

_____

_____

_____

4. _____

_____

_____

_____

5. _____

_____

_____

_____

Talk It Over

Discuss these questions as a class.

1. Why do you think some fads last for years? What features might make a fad like the Slinky or Silly Putty a classic?
2. Most of the fads in the article (the Pet Rock, the Slinky, Silly Putty, the Hula Hoop) are toys. Why do you think the toy market has so many fads?

Do Some Research

Use the Internet or library to find some interesting information about scooters. Share the information from your research with your classmates.

The Price of Power

The buying and selling of energy is big business. In fact, it's probably the biggest business. Since oil is the most common form of energy, some economists think oil fuels the world's economy.

Before You Read

A Discuss these questions with a partner.

1. Why do you think oil is so expensive? How can people reduce their dependence on oil?
2. Can you think of other forms of energy that could be used instead of oil?
3. Have you ever seen or driven a car that runs on something other than gas? If so, what did it use for fuel?

✓ **Skimming for the Main Idea**

B Skim the article one time. Then circle the number of the statement you think describes the main idea.

1. A new kind of car, called a Flex car, is gaining popularity in South America.
2. Because oil is so expensive, scientists are exploring new ways to meet our energy needs.
3. People around the world already turn the sun's strength into usable energy.

C Learn the meanings of the following words and phrase before you read the article.

fuel (1)   vehicle (4)

run out of (1)   stinks (6)

alternative (2)   convert (7)

flexible (4)

THE PRICE OF POWER

Selling New Kinds of Energy

By Andrea Delbanco

1 Americans use more than 21 million barrels of oil every day to power their farms, factories, and cities, to fuel their cars, and to heat their homes. The world won't run out of oil anytime soon, but oil is an expensive source of energy. Many experts worry that it will soon become too expensive to obtain oil from the world's underground oil supplies. This will make oil prices even higher. As a result, scientists are searching for other ways to meet the world's energy needs. They are looking for reliable ways that make sense economically.

2 Alternative solutions for supplying energy, such as capturing the power of the sun and wind, are already being used all over the world. There is a rapidly growing search for renewable energy sources (forms of energy that can be produced as quickly as they are used). Here are some creative ways that we can turn nature's power into energy at a reasonable cost.

Water Power

3 Running water is an important energy source. People around the world use dams to control rivers in order to produce electricity. But the future of water power may be in using the energy of ocean waves to make electricity. Tom Denniss has studied the ocean's power for many years. His company, Energetech, is working on the best ways to use wave power. One project in Australia uses a floating power plant to turn the motion of ocean waves into electricity. Energetech has projects in Rhode Island and Israel, too. Denniss believes the ocean's strong waves will soon be turning on our lights.

Sugar Power

4 Drivers in Brazil are filling up their cars with fuel that comes from sugarcane. A new kind of car, called a *Flex* car, is gaining popularity in the South American country. *Flex* is short for *flexible*, which describes the vehicle's fuel needs. They run on either regular gasoline or ethanol, a kind of alcohol that can be produced from sugarcane. Sugarcane is a crop that is grown all over Brazil.

5 Flex cars look and work like regular vehicles. Volkswagen, Ford, Fiat, and GM all produce Flex lines. Recently, sales of Flex vehicles were higher than sales of gasoline models in Brazil. Alfred Szwarc is an energy

consultant in Brazil. He said, "People see Flex cars as the cars of the future."

Flex cars can use either regular gasoline or a kind of alcohol produced from sugarcane.

Don't Waste "Waste"

6   Animal waste stinks, but it can also be useful. Machines called *biogas digesters* turn animal waste into a power supply. Here's how they work: Farmers collect animal waste and put it into a large digester, or tank. Inside the digester, methane gas is separated from the waste. The methane gas can then be used to heat homes and make electricity. This technology has been used for many years in places such as Nepal, China, and India.

Digesters keep getting easier to use and less expensive. One digester that produces gas for cooking costs only $180. Last year, more than 1,700 digesters were installed on farms in China's Yunnan province. Digesters are also being used in some village schools to make sure that students' waste is not wasted. Biogas keeps the lights turned on at Myeka High School in South Africa.

The Power of the Sun

7   People around the world already turn sunshine into usable energy. Special solar panels are put on roofs to convert sunshine into electricity that can be used to run factories, heat water, or cool homes. Solar panels can be used on smaller things, too. Backpacks with solar panels that can power up cell phones and MP3 players are already on the market. Scientists are also working on clothing with solar panels. One day, you may be able to plug your laptop into a solar cell battery on your jacket—as long as the sun is shining!

After You Read

Comprehension Check

One quart (1.2 liters) of oil can pollute about 250 gallons (1,200 liters) of drinking water.

A Circle the letter of the correct answer.

1. Which is NOT an example of renewable energy?
   a. water
   b. oil
   c. ethanol

2. The price of oil has _____.
   a. gone up
   b. remained the same
   c. gone down

3. What are dams used for?
   a. to use the motion of ocean waves
   b. to monitor the rise and fall of tides
   c. to control rivers to produce electricity

4. Which is true about biogas digesters?
   a. They are becoming easier to use and less expensive.
   b. They used to be easier to use and less expensive.
   c. They keep getting easier to use and more expensive.

5. Cell phones and MP3 players that use _____ are already on the market.
   a. running water
   b. ethanol gas
   c. solar power

6. Which statement is true about Flex cars?
   a. They look and work like regular cars.
   b. They can use only regular gasoline.
   c. They haven't been used yet.

✓ **Identifying Facts and Opinions**

B Decide if each statement is a fact or an opinion. Check (✓) the correct box.

	Fact	Opinion
1. The ocean's strong waves will soon be turning on our lights.		
2. Sugarcane is a crop that is grown all over Brazil.		
3. Machines called biogas digesters turn animal waste into a power supply.		
4. One day, you may be able to plug your laptop into a solar cell battery on your jacket.		
5. People see Flex cars as the cars of the future.		
6. Last year, more than 1,700 digesters were installed on farms in China's Yunnan province.		

Vocabulary Practice

A Complete each sentence with the correct word or phrase.

alternative   run out of
convert   stinks
flexible   vehicles
fuel

1. You need a special license to drive _____ like trucks and taxis.

2. This milk _____. Let's throw it out.

3. Gasoline is the most common type of _____ for cars.

4. Solar power is a(n) _____ source of energy.

5. These cars are _____. They run on either gas or ethanol.

6. We need to stop at a gas station before we _____ gas.

7. Biogas digesters _____ animal waste into a power supply.

B Answer each question with *Yes* or *No*.

1. If you <u>run out of</u> gas in your car, does your car stop? _____
2. Can ethanol be used as an <u>alternative</u> to gasoline? _____
3. If some food in the refrigerator <u>stinks</u>, does it smell good? _____
4. Are methane gas, gasoline, and oil examples of <u>fuel</u>? _____
5. If your schedule is <u>flexible</u>, can you make changes to it? _____
6. Are buses, cars, trucks, and vans all examples of <u>vehicles</u>? _____
7. Can the wind be <u>converted</u> into electricity? _____

SKILL FOR SUCCESS

Understanding Word Parts: The Suffixes *-able* and *-ible*
The suffixes *-able* and *-ible* form adjectives from verbs. For example, *predict* (a verb) becomes *predictable* (an adjective). *Flex* (a verb) becomes *flexible* (an adjective).

C Complete the chart. Add the suffix *-able* or *-ible* to each verb to make an adjective. Use your dictionary for help with spelling.

Verb	Adjective
1. profit	
2. use	
3. solve	
4. convert	
5. renew	
6. predict	
7. exhaust	

D Complete each sentence with the correct adjective from the chart in Exercise C.

1. Resources that will be used up completely and disappear are called _____ resources.

2. Wind and wave power are _____ forms of energy that can be produced as quickly as they are used.

3. We know that the price of oil is going to continue rising in the future. It is a(n) _____ situation.

4. The problem of Earth's energy shortage is _____. I'm certain we can come up with a solution.

5. People around the world already turn the sun's strength into _____ energy.

6. Animal waste is _____. It can be changed into simpler substances, like methane gas.

7. Denniss hopes his company, Energetech, will be _____.

Talk It Over

Discuss these questions as a class.

1. Do you think people can save much money by using alternative energy sources?
2. Do you know anyone who owns a hybrid car (a car that can use either electricity or gasoline)? Why do you think hybrid cars are becoming so popular?
3. Do you or does anyone you know have a house with solar panels or any other energy-saving techniques?
4. What can we do in our everyday lives to reduce the amount of oil we use?

Smells Sell!

Before You Read

A Discuss these questions with a partner.

1. Are you sensitive to smells? Do you have a good sense of smell?
2. What are some things you think smell good? What are some things you think smell bad?
3. Do certain smells bring back good memories for you? If so, what past events do you associate with good smells?
4. How do you think smells can be used to sell things?

✓ **Using Background Knowledge**

B Think about what you know about the sense of smell. You are going to read about the sense of smell. Check (✓) the statements about this topic that you think are true. Then compare answers with a partner.

☐ 1. The sense of smell helps us remember things.
☐ 2. Our sense of smell is not very strong.
☐ 3. Store owners use smells to influence customers.
☐ 4. Scientists study the effects of certain smells.
☐ 5. Some smells can make us feel hungry.
☐ 6. Our sense of smell can help us avoid danger.

C Learn the meanings of the following words and phrase before you read the article.

led by the nose (2)	tricky (4)
fake (2)	volunteers (5)
entice (2)	proof (5)
fragrance (4)	

Smells Sell!

by Melinda Crow

1   Scientists have been studying the power of smells for many years. They have learned that more than any of our other four senses, our sense of smell can change our mood and help us remember things. For example, if you are told to think about popcorn, you would probably remember its smell. And then you might remember a movie you saw while eating it. Our sense of smell also helps us avoid danger—like when our sense of smell warns us of fire. And smells can make you feel hungry, from just one whiff of food.

The Power of Smell

2   Because the sense of smell is so powerful, store owners use smells to sell products. Businesses spend thousands of dollars to scent their stores. They hope the odors will get people inside the store and put them in the mood to buy. They also hope the smell will help customers remember the store later, so they'll come back again. Suppose you are in a grocery store looking for your favorite kind of cereal to buy. Suddenly, you smell chocolate chip cookies. They smell scrumptious. You forget all about buying cereal and go to the bakery section. Guess what! You were being led by the nose. You walked into a trap—an odor trap! The smell was fake. The odor was cooked up by scientists in a lab. Then it was spread by the store's owners to entice you to come to the bakery section.

3   Using smells to sell products isn't new. In 1966, one company added the smell of lemon to its dish detergent. They wanted people to think the soap contained "natural" cleaners. It worked! Food companies discovered ways to make microwaveable foods smell good before they're cooked. They scent the packages.

Spreading Smells

4   Store designer J'Amy Owens uses "fragrance planning" as part of her store design. She believes each store should have its own special smell. For example, for a children's clothing store, Owens used the smell of cinnamon and apples. She hopes shoppers will think the children's clothes are as American as apple pie[1]. Owens spreads the store scents secretly. She soaks[2] little balls in fragrance and hides them in light fixtures and heating pipes. She also puts some in a small heater to warm up the fragrance. A fan in the heater spreads the smell throughout the store. Sometimes she uses computer-controlled machines to spread the smell. But getting the right amount of odor in the air can be tricky. When one store owner first started using peach fragrance in his store, the whole store ended up smelling like a peach farm.

[1] **as American as apple pie** – typical of the American way of life

[2] **soak** – to cover with liquid for a period of time

Is There Proof?

5 Do the smells really work? Dr. Alan Hirsch is an expert on smell. He thinks using smells works. Hirsch says that it doesn't take a lot of smell to affect you. Store owners can lure you to the candy aisle—even if you don't realize you are smelling candy. Dr. Hirsch has done some interesting experiments to test the effects of smell on customers. In one experiment, he took thirty-one people to a sneaker store that smelled slightly like flowers. Later, he took another group of volunteers to the same store, but with no flower odor. Dr. Hirsch found that 84 percent of the shoppers were more likely to buy sneakers when the store was scented. He also found that it didn't matter if the people liked the smell or not. "Whether the volunteers liked the flower scent or not didn't matter," Hirsch says. "Some reported that they hated the smell. But they still were more likely to buy the shoes in the scented room." That's pretty good proof that smells influence purchasing behavior.

The Smell Debate

6 Using smells to influence customer behavior is a controversial issue. Some people think it is a good idea, but not everyone does.

In fact, using smells scares a lot of people. They say the stores are using a kind of brainwashing[3], which they call "smell-washing." Other people disagree. Dr. Hirsch says stores already use background music and special lighting. "Why not smells?" Some businesspeople predict that store smells will be as common as Muzak.

New Uses for Smells

7 New uses for smells are created every day. One bank, for example, gives customers coupons for car loans. To get people to take out a loan, bank officials plan to scent the coupons with the fresh leather smell of a new car. In Australia, companies put sweat odor on unpaid bills. Since some people sweat when they're scared, this smell might remind them of when they are frightened. And they'll pay the bills right away.

8 Smell scientists are working on other new ways to use smells. Soon TVs and computers may produce smells. Alarm clocks will scent your bedroom with an aroma designed to wake you up. Scientists are even working on ways to keep garbage from stinking. And researchers think scents might help students learn more easily.

[3] **brainwashing** – making someone believe something that is not true by using force, confusing him or her, or continuously repeating it

After You Read

Comprehension Check

A Read these statements. If a statement is true according to the article, write *T* on the line. If it is false, write *F*.

_____ 1. The sense of smell can change your mood and help you remember things.

_____ 2. Because the sense of smell is so powerful, some businesses use it to sell products.

_____ 3. In the future, store smells might be as common as soft music.

_____ 4. It takes a large amount of a certain smell to affect a customer.

_____ 5. It is always easy to get the right amount of odor in the air.

_____ 6. Some people oppose the idea of using smells to influence customers.

_____ 7. Using smells to sell products is a new idea.

_____ 8. New uses for smells are being developed all the time.

SKILL FOR SUCCESS

Identifying Supporting Information
You have learned that a paragraph usually has one main idea. Main ideas are **supported with facts, reasons, and examples.** After you identify the main idea, look for information that supports it. Understanding the relationship between the main idea and the supporting sentences will improve your reading comprehension.

B Read these statements. Write *M* in front of the statement that expresses the main idea of the paragraph. Write *S* in front of the statements that give supporting information.

1. Paragraph 1

_M_ More than any of our other four senses, our sense of smell can change our mood and help us remember things.

_S_ For example, if you are told to think about popcorn, you would probably remember its smell.

_S_ Our sense of smell also helps us avoid danger—like fire.

_S_ And smells can make you feel hungry, from just one whiff of food.

2. Paragraph 2

_____ Because the sense of smell is so powerful, store owners use smells to sell products.

_____ They hope the odors will get people inside the store and put them in the mood to buy.

_____ They also hope the smell will help customers remember the store later, so they'll come back again.

3. Paragraph 3

_____ Food companies discovered ways to make microwaveable foods smell good before they're cooked.

_____ Using smells to sell products isn't new.

_____ In 1966, one company added the smell of lemon to its dish detergent.

4. Paragraph 4

_____ For example, for a children's clothing store, Owens used the smell of cinnamon and apples.

_____ Owens uses "fragrance planning" as part of her store design.

_____ Owens spreads the store scents secretly.

5. Paragraph 5

_____ In one experiment, Hirsch took thirty-one people to a sneaker store that smelled slightly like flowers.

_____ Hirsch has done some interesting experiments to test the effects of smell on customers.

_____ Hirsch also found that it didn't matter if the people liked the smell or not.

6. Paragraph 6

_____ Using smells to influence customer behavior is a controversial issue.

_____ In fact, using smells scares a lot of people.

_____ Some people think it is a good idea, but not everyone does.

7. Paragraph 7

_____ In Australia, companies put sweat odor on unpaid bills.

_____ New uses for smells are created every day.

_____ One bank, for example, gives customers coupons for car loans.

Vocabulary Practice

A Match each word or phrase with the correct definition.

Word or Phrase	Definition
_____ 1. fake	a. to attract someone or persuade someone to do something
_____ 2. entice	b. difficult to deal with
_____ 3. led by the nose	c. a pleasant smell
_____ 4. fragrance	d. facts or information that show that something is true
_____ 5. volunteer	e. not real
_____ 6. proof	f. someone who offers to do something without pay
_____ 7. tricky	g. controlled someone and made them do what you wanted

B Circle the letter of the correct answer.

1. Which is true about a <u>fake</u> fur coat?
   a. It is not made from real fur. b. It is made from real fur.
2. If someone tells you the directions to the hotel are <u>tricky</u>, they are probably _____.
   a. easy to follow b. difficult to follow
3. If a commercial <u>enticed</u> you to buy a new product, the commercial was _____.
   a. successful b. unsuccessful
4. If you are a <u>volunteer</u> for the fire department, you _____.
   a. work there without getting paid b. get paid to help put out fires
5. If someone <u>leads you by the nose</u>, you _____.
   a. make your own decision b. do what someone else wants
6. What could you use as <u>proof</u> of your age?
   a. your driver's license b. the money in your wallet
7. If something has the <u>fragrance</u> of flowers, it _____.
   a. looks like a flower b. smells like a flower

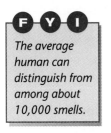

The average human can distinguish from among about 10,000 smells.

C Cross out the word in each group that does not belong.

1. fake	phony	real	false
2. evidence	proof	confirmation	confusion
3. odor	sound	fragrance	aroma

| 4. difficult | complicated | easy | tricky |
| 5. entice | tempt | persuade | lead by the nose |

✓ **Using Context Clues**

D Using context clues, circle the letter of the definition or synonym for each underlined word or phrase. Then compare answers with a partner. Do not use a dictionary.

1. Suddenly, you smell chocolate chip cookies. They smell <u>scrumptious</u>. You forget all about buying cereal and go to the bakery section.
   a. terrible
   b. delicious
   c. unhappy

2. And smells can make you feel hungry, from just one <u>whiff</u> of food.
   a. touch
   b. sight
   c. smell

3. The smell was fake. The odor was <u>cooked up</u> by scientists in a lab.
   a. created
   b. sold
   c. printed

4. Using smells to influence customer behavior is a <u>controversial</u> issue. Some people think it is a good idea, but not everyone does.
   a. costing a lot of money
   b. having a good smell
   c. causing disagreement

5. Soon TVs and computers may produce smells. Alarm clocks will scent your bedroom with an <u>aroma</u> designed to wake you up.
   a. loud noise
   b. pleasant smell
   c. unusual voice

6. Store owners can <u>lure</u> you to the candy aisle—even if you don't realize you are smelling candy.
   a. persuade you to go
   b. want you to go
   c. help you to go

✓ **Learning Idioms: Expressions with the Word** *Smell*

E Study these idioms based on the word *smell*. Then complete the conversation that follows, using each idiom only once.

1. *Smells fishy* refers to a situation you think is bad or dishonest.
2. *Smell a rat* means "to be suspicious" or "to believe that something is wrong about a situation, especially that someone is being dishonest."
3. *Pass the smell test* means "to be acceptable."
4. *Wake up and smell the coffee* means "to pay attention and do something about a situation."
5. *Come out smelling like a rose* means "to end something positively."

A: Did you hear that the mayor is being accused of stealing money from the city treasury?

B: I read something about it. But I don't know if I believe it. I think something about the situation _____.

1.

A: Me, too. Personally, I think the mayor is innocent. I think his assistant is lying about what happened. The more I read about it, the more I

_____.

2.

B: I think you're right. I think it's time for people to

_____ and realize something is not right. But

3.

let's see what happens during the investigation.

Later:

A: Were you surprised at what happened during the investigation? The assistant's story certainly didn't _____. The

4.

police knew he was lying.

B: People were too quick to blame the mayor. But look what happened. They thought the mayor was guilty, but in the end he was completely innocent. The mayor _____ after all.

5.

Talk It Over

1. Do you think it's OK for store owners to use fake smells to influence your mood?
2. Can you think of any stores you go to that use smells to sell their products? If so, what do they sell? What do you buy?
3. In what ways is using smells similar to using background music?

Tie It All Together

Discussion

Read these quotations about business, and discuss the related questions in a small group.

1. B. C. Forbes was a financial journalist and the founder of *Forbes* business magazine. He said, "Don't forget until too late that the business of life is not business, but living."

   What do you think this quote means? Do you agree with Forbes's point of view? Do you know people who lead their lives as though they think work is all there is to life? What are some of the reasons people might do this? In English, we call these people *workaholics*. Are you one of these people?

2. Henry Ford, founder of the Ford Motor Company, once said, "A business that makes nothing but money is a poor business."

   Do you agree? Why or why not?

3. Business is concerned with persuading people to buy. As a result, a lot of money is spent on marketing, advertising, and promotion. The owner of a cosmetics company said, "We don't sell lipstick; we buy customers."

   Do you ever feel manipulated when you buy something? If so, when?

Just for Fun

The letters to the word *controversial* are in the boxes. Make as many words as you can using these letters. The letter *A* must occur in every word you make. Write your words on the lines below.

C	T	R	
R	S	O	A
V	E	N	
O	I	L	

1. _____   4. _____   7. _____   10. _____

2. _____   5. _____   8. _____   11. _____

3. _____   6. _____   9. _____   12. _____

Teen Trends

You will see a video about teen fashion trends. The video examines how a fad begins and gains popularity. How do you think certain styles become popular? Why do you think they stop being popular?

A Study these words and phrases. Then watch the video.

alpha-teen	cottage industry	spontaneous
at the cradle	flattered	vintage
cool	jumped the shark	

B Read these questions and then watch the video again. Write an answer to each question.

1. According to the video, does a particular style become a trend very quickly or over time? Give an example.

   _____

   _____

2. Who is Malcolm Gladwell? What does he mean when he says, "Trends are a virus"?

   _____

   _____

3. According to the video, what is an example of a trend that relates to speech, not fashion? How did it begin?

   _____

   _____

4. What is an "it girl"? Why does the fashion industry rely on an army of "it girls"?

   _____

   _____

C Discuss these questions with a partner or in a small group.

1. What trends do you remember from your childhood? What are some trends now?
2. Do you think of yourself as an influencer? How much do trends influence you?

Reader's Journal

Think about the topics and ideas you have read about and discussed in this unit. Pick a topic from the list, one of the discussion questions in the unit, or an idea of your own. Write about it for ten to twenty minutes.

- a fad that interests you
- the importance of developing alternative energy sources
- things that affect your purchasing decisions

Vocabulary Self-Test

Complete each sentence with the correct word or phrase.

A
fragrance	invested	mood	vehicle
fuel	make a mint	tricky	

1. It will be _____ to get just the right smell. We don't want it to be too weak, but we certainly don't want the store to smell like a perfume factory!

2. Do you have a license to drive a(n) _____ such as a motorcycle?

3. I _____ some money in my brother-in-law's new business. I hope I _____ as a result.

4. Most fresh flowers have a wonderful _____.

5. The team was in a great _____ after they won the game.

6. Don't leave your car engine on when you are not driving. It wastes _____.

B
alternative	practical	selling like hotcakes	volunteer
enticed	run out of	tips	word of mouth

1. I hope I can finish this project before I _____ time.

2. That ad has _____ a lot of people to buy a new car.

3. The main road to the mall is closed today. We're going to have to find a(n) _____ road.

4. _____ is the best way to find a good dentist.

5. We have to be _____ and not spend so much money.

6. Felipe gave me some good _____ on how to take better pictures.

7. More than 500 people _____ at the museum during their free time.

8. The hats in Dina's new store are very cute. Everyone wants one. They are _____.

C catching on   fake   led by the nose   stinks
    convert   flexible   proof

1. You must show _____ that you purchased the item when you return it to a store.

2. Delma told me she wants to buy a _____ fur coat.

3. Hybrid cars are _____. You see them everywhere.

4. We need more space. We are going to _____ our garage into an office.

5. After he eats, my dog's breath _____.

6. She didn't know what she was agreeing to. She was being _____ by her boss.

7. I like working with Miao. She is always _____ and open to new ideas.

TUNE IN TO TV

Television has been called the machine that brings the world into your home. Whether you are in the mood to learn, laugh, cry, think, or relax, you can usually find something to watch on TV. This unit presents a brief history of TV and discusses how TV reflects and influences society.

Points to Ponder

A Check (✔) the statements that are true for you. Then compare answers with a partner.

☐ 1. TV stimulates my mind.
☐ 2. I wouldn't mind not having a TV.
☐ 3. Watching TV helps me relax.
☐ 4. I would rather read than watch TV.
☐ 5. I like to watch TV while I'm doing other things.
☐ 6. TV commercials influence what I buy.
☐ 7. I would rather watch commercial-free television.
☐ 8. TV programs are getting better.
☐ 9. Watching TV is usually a waste of time.
☐ 10. I like TV commercials.

B Think about these questions and discuss them in a small group.

1. On the average, how many hours do you watch TV each day? Each week?
2. Do you like to have the television on in the background even if you aren't really watching it?

The Early Days and Beyond

Before You Read

A Discuss these questions with a partner.

1. Does everyone you know have a TV?
2. Do your parents or grandparents ever talk about their life before TV? If so, what do they say?
3. How do you think your life would be different without TV?

✓ **Skimming for the Main Idea**

B Skim the article one time. Circle the number of the sentence that tells the main idea of the article.

1. In the early 1930s, telecasts were usually short and simple.
2. Franklin D. Roosevelt became the first president to appear on television.
3. Television has changed a lot since it was invented.

C Learn the meanings of the following words and phrases before you read the article.

transmitted (1)   brought a halt to (4)
trial and error (1)   craze (4)
big hit (3)   links (8)

The Early Days and Beyond

1   The earliest experiments in television took place in the late nineteenth century. After the invention of the telephone in the 1870s, scientists began to wonder if pictures—like sound—could be transmitted through the air. However, it took many years of trial and error to get things right because televisions are complicated machines.

2   The earliest television shows were often called telecasts or broadcasts. They were usually just pictures transmitted from one place to another. However, in 1928, WGY, in Schenectady, New York, became the first regularly operating television station in the United States. It simulcast[1] programs with a radio station for half an hour, three days a week. People watched the pictures on a television and listened to the sounds from their radio.

3   In the early 1930s, telecasts were usually short and simple. Not many people had television sets to receive the pictures anyway. In 1936, only about 200 television sets were in use worldwide. But in 1939, television was displayed at the World's Fair in New York City and was a big hit. That year, Franklin D. Roosevelt became the first president to appear on television.

4   By the early 1940s, there were twenty-three television stations in the United States. But soon World War II brought a halt to the television industry. After the war, however, the TV craze really began. By 1947, there were 170,000 TV sets in the United States.

By the end of 1948, there were 2.5 million television sets. Two years later, that number had increased to 10 million TV sets.

5   Only fifty years ago, watching television was a totally different experience from what it is today. Then, the average family watched only black-and-white shows on a 7-inch screen. There were no remote

control[2] devices to change channels from the comfort of a sofa. Programs were aired only a few hours every evening.

6   However, the popularity of television pushed scientists to keep thinking up new ways to improve it. And they did. Color telecasts began in 1953. The first color TVs were too expensive for most people, and it took over a decade for color TVs to become popular. But once they did, color TVs were everywhere, and soon all programs were produced and broadcast in color. On July 20, 1969, 600 million people watched the first TV transmission from the moon. Sony introduced the first home videocassette recorder in 1976, and soon people were recording their favorite shows and watching them whenever they wanted. They were also able to rent movies and

---

[1] **simulcast** – to broadcast two programs at the same time

[2] **remote control** – equipment that you use to control a radio, television, toy, etc., from a distance

watch them at home on their own TVs. In 1979, 300 million television sets were in operation worldwide. By 1996, the number had increased to 1 billion TV sets worldwide.

7 As the twentieth century drew to a close, TV improved in many ways. There were larger screens, better reception, and more varied programming. People used remote controls and watched cable TV and digital TV.

8 Today, television is a communications system that links the far corners of the globe. TV is so much a part of our lives that it's almost impossible to imagine a world without it. At any time of day or night, we can tune in to the latest news from around the world. We can watch presentations of the arts, investigations of crimes, live sporting events, and documentaries that explore the world. We can learn how to cook gourmet meals, plant a vegetable garden, decorate our homes, and speak Spanish or Japanese. Or if we just want to relax, we can watch a movie on a network channel or rent a video from a cable channel. And who knows what the future will bring? ■

After You Read

Comprehension Check

A Circle the letter of the correct answer.

1. Television really became popular _____.
   a. before World War II
   b. during the late nineteenth century
   c. after World War II

2. At first, the telecasts were _____.
   a. long and complicated
   b. short and simple
   c. broadcast in color

3. _____ was the first president of the United States to appear on TV.
   a. John F. Kennedy
   b. Richard Nixon
   c. Franklin D. Roosevelt

4. Only fifty years ago, watching TV was _____ what it is today.
   a. very different from
   b. somewhat different from
   c. almost the same as

5. The main purpose of "The Early Days and Beyond" is to _____.
   a. give a history of television
   b. explain how television works
   c. discuss why television programming is so bad

✓ **Scanning for Information**

B Scan the article for the information to complete the paragraph. Work as quickly as possible.

Although scientists first began experimenting with television in the late _____, it was not until _____ that the world's first
         1.   2.
real television station showed programs regularly. Back then, televisions broadcast the pictures, but the sound came from radios. Very few people owned televisions, and shows in the _____ were short and
                                     3.
simple. In _____, television was a big hit at the World's Fair. By
                4.
1947, there were _____ TV sets in the United States. By the end
                    5.
of the next year, the number jumped to _____. TVs were
                             6.
catching on quickly, and two years later, the number reached more than
_____. Television's popularity grew, and in _____, the
       7.   8.
first color telecasts began. By _____, there were 1 billion TV sets
                               9.
worldwide.

SKILL FOR SUCCESS ✓

Using Graphic Organizers: Making a Timeline
Remember that **graphic organizers** help you organize information. **Timelines** are another kind of graphic organizer. Timelines show important dates and events.

C Make a timeline about the history of television. Include the dates and events you think are important. Find some information about the history of TV in your country and include it on the timeline.

1928	

WGY became the world's
first regularly operating
television studio

A Circle the letter of the word or phrase that is closest in meaning to the underlined word or phrase in each sentence.

1. After the invention of the telephone in the 1870s, scientists began to wonder if pictures—like sound—could be <u>transmitted</u> through the air.
   a. bought
   b. sent
   c. increased

2. However, it took many years of <u>trial and error</u> to get things right because televisions are complicated machines.
   a. trying different things and learning from mistakes
   b. going to court and talking to a judge
   c. returning damaged machines

3. In 1939, television was displayed at the World's Fair in New York City and was a <u>big hit</u>.
   a. strong punch
   b. failure
   c. success

4. By the early 1940s, there were twenty-three television stations in the United States. But soon World War II <u>brought a halt to</u> the television industry.
   a. invented
   b. stopped
   c. battled

5. After the war, however, the TV <u>craze</u> really began.
   a. very popular activity
   b. slow movement
   c. high cost

6. Today, television is a communications system that <u>links</u> the far corners of the globe.
   a. produces
   b. separates
   c. connects

B Cross out the word or phrase in each group that does not belong.

1. fad	craze	trend	trial
2. joins	connects	separates	links
3. halt	stop	end	grow
4. failure	hit	winner	success

5. transmit   hold   send   broadcast

6. experiment   test   failure   trial and error

SKILL FOR SUCCESS ✔

Learning Homonyms

Homonyms are words that are spelled the same or sound the same but have different meanings. Consider the word *hit*.

> *The TV show was a big hit.* (In this sentence, *hit* means "something that is very successful.")
> *It isn't nice to hit your dog.* (In this sentence, *hit* means "to strike someone or something with your hand.")

Understanding the different meanings of homonyms will help you become a more fluent reader.

C Read these sentences. Write the meaning and part of speech of each underlined word. You may need to use your dictionary.

1. a. The Internet <u>links</u> people from around the world.
      Meaning: _____*connects*_____
      Part of speech: _____*verb*_____
   b. If you click on this <u>link</u>, you will get to my Website.
      Meaning: _____
      Part of speech: _____

2. a. We need to <u>tune</u> our piano. It sounds terrible.
      Meaning: _____
      Part of speech: _____
   b. I love the <u>tune</u> he's playing on his guitar.
      Meaning: _____
      Part of speech: _____

3. a. My new TV <u>set</u> has great stereo sound.
      Meaning: _____
      Part of speech: _____
   b. You can <u>set</u> the VCR to start recording at anytime you choose.
      Meaning: _____
      Part of speech: _____

4. a. My TV has a thirty-inch <u>screen</u>.
      Meaning: _____
      Part of speech: _____
   b. I usually <u>screen</u> my calls while I'm having dinner with my family.
      Meaning: _____
      Part of speech: _____

5. **a.** I'm going to <u>record</u> the soccer game on TV.
   Meaning: _____
   Part of speech: _____

   b. Do you have a <u>record</u> of your purchase?
   Meaning: _____
   Part of speech: _____

6. **a.** The new comedy will <u>air</u> tonight for the first time.
   Meaning: _____
   Part of speech: _____

   b. The <u>air</u> we breathe should be clean and free of pollutants.
   Meaning: _____
   Part of speech: _____

7. **a.** He saw a commercial for a new kind of <u>watch</u> on TV and decided to buy one.
   Meaning: _____
   Part of speech: _____

   b. Would you like to <u>watch</u> a movie on TV tonight?
   Meaning: _____
   Part of speech: _____

✓ **Using Graphic Organizers: Making a Chart**
Read the short passage about praise for and criticism of TV. Then complete the chart that follows with information from the passage. (Choose three points for each side.)

TV Has Changed Our Lives—for Better or for Worse

Television as we know it is only about sixty years old. Yet it's so much a part of our lives that it seems as if it always existed. Some people think that the years before television were a better time. They claim that families talked more and did more things together. Before television, they say, people read more books. They used their imaginations more fully. They got more outdoor exercise. But others disagree. They claim that life after television is better because television is a powerful educational tool. It informs us of events in the world, from a famine in Africa to a local fire, in a matter of minutes. Television today also helps shape our opinions about everything from politics to fashion. With television in our lives, we can understand how other people live, work, and struggle.

Some people credit television with being a great teacher. Others blame TV for the poor reading and writing skills of our population. Television gets praise for helping us understand the people of the world. But people also say it is destroying family life. People applaud television for keeping us informed about the political issues of the day. But it can also make us lazy by giving us only "news briefs" that are too short to tell the whole story.

People will probably continue to argue about television's value. But everyone agrees that it is one of the most significant inventions of the twentieth century. Even people who love television love to criticize it. As one writer put it, "Television influences everyone, and it pleases no one fully."

The Television Debate		
	Praise for Television	**Criticism of Television**
1.		
2.		
3.		

Debate the Issue   Some people think television has a positive effect on society. Other people think it has a negative effect. Which side are you on? Work in a small group. Take turns sharing and explaining your opinions.

Dora the Explorer Leads the Way

Before You Read

A Discuss these questions with a partner.

1. Look at the picture of Dora in the article. Have you ever seen the show *Dora the Explorer*? Do you know what languages she speaks?
2. Do you think it is important for TV shows to reflect the multicultural nature of society?
3. Do you think watching TV can help you learn a new language? How?

B Learn the meanings of the following words and phrase before you read the article.

character (1)   animated (4)
episode (1)   pilot (7)
themes (2)   heroine (9)
prime time (2)   spin-off (9)
diversity (2)

✓ **Previewing and Predicting**

C Preview the article by looking at the title, subtitle, headings, and photo. Skim the first paragraph and the first sentence of the other paragraphs. Think about the words above. Make some predictions about the content of the article. Write your ideas on the lines.

_____

_____

_____

DORA THE EXPLORER LEADS THE WAY

Latino Characters Becoming Common in Kids' TV

1 Have you ever heard of Dora the Explorer? She is a seven-year-old TV cartoon character

loved by children around the world. Almost everyone in Dora's world speaks fluent English and Spanish. Her adventures are accompanied by salsa rhythms, and young TV viewers love the mix. Each episode of *Dora the Explorer* starts with Dora waving good-bye to her mother (Mami) and father (Papi) and running off into the jungle. *Dora the Explorer* was the top-rated preschool program for four years.

2 If you want to see television shows that feature Latino characters and themes, don't look to prime-time TV. Most of the shows on prime time overlook Latinos, the nation's largest ethnic group. Today, most Latino TV shows are children's programs. "These programs are making diversity a natural part of kids' understanding of the world around them," said Phillip C. Serrato, a professor of children's literature at California State University at San Diego.

New Latino Characters on TV

3 In the past, there were very few multicultural children's TV programs. The Public Broadcasting System (PBS) show *Sesame Street* was really the only example.

For thirty-seven years, *Sesame Street* has included Latino characters, including a Puerto Rican family and a Mexican "monster" named Rosita. But now PBS Kids has more Latino offerings. For example, *Dragon Tales* highlights Latino issues and includes a character named Enrique, an immigrant who is Puerto Rican and Colombian. The show *Jay Jay the Jet Plane* added a new bilingual airplane named Lina.

4 The Disney Channel is also planning to feature Latino characters in a show called *Handy Manny*. It is a cartoon centered on a bilingual handyman[1] named Manny Garcia. He uses his Spanish-speaking "talking" tools to do his work. The Cartoon Network has *Mucha Lucha*, a Mexican wrestling cartoon. And Scholastic Entertainment has the animated show *Maya & Miguel*. This show is produced by Scholastic Entertainment and aimed at Spanish-speaking kids just starting school. "All the characters are bilingual to varying degrees," said Deborah Forte, Scholastic's president. "Abuela (Grandma) Elena speaks Spanish. The kids speak much more English, especially out in the streets, but they pepper it with Spanish. We studied the way families spoke, and this was the way many of them did it."

What's Driving the Trend?

5 Producers[2] say demographics are driving the trend of Latino TV shows. (Demographics are characteristics such as age and ethnicity of the people who live in a particular area.)

---

[1] **handyman** – someone who makes and repairs things

[2] **producer** – someone who controls the preparation of a play, movie, or TV show

The 2000 census[3] showed that Latino communities are the United States's fastest-growing group. And the biggest Latino age group is infants to preschoolers. Studies in the late 1990s showed Latino youth almost never saw themselves on-screen and that made them feel society ignored them. A 1999 Annenberg Public Policy Center report said that "Latino American preschoolers ought to and deserve to see greater representation of their own culture."

6   Cyma Zarghami is the president of Nickelodeon Television[4]. She said the message got through. "It felt like an audience was being underserved." After reading the studies, the producers at Nickelodeon came up with the show about Dora. The show first appeared in 1999 and quickly became a big hit. It's now shown in 125 countries.

7   Brown Johnson is Nickelodeon's executive creative director. She made sure that every detail of Dora's appearance, her family background, and her speech reflected her Latino heritage. Johnson said, "In the original *Dora* pilot, she had green eyes, but we changed them to brown eyes and made her skin a little darker," she said. "That was more appropriate."

8   Experts urged them to make the show's songs more Latino and to incorporate Spanish. *Dora* was the first mainstream show to try to teach Spanish by blending Spanish into natural conversation, as opposed to translating individual vocabulary words.

9   "Here was a show that had a Latina heroine who was young and spoke Spanish in a cartoon," said Clara E. Rodriguez, a sociologist at Fordham University who briefly advised the producers. Soon, Dora's cousin Diego Marquez, who rescues animals, was a popular guest on her show, and in October the spin-off *Go, Diego, Go!* became an instant hit.

10   Lisa Raymond-Tolan of Brooklyn, who is white, said her preschool-age son adores Diego. "Even though we're not Hispanic, my son loves learning the language. . . . It teaches him there's a bigger world full of wonderful things."

TV's Marketing Power Targets Kids

11   Nickelodeon hopes sales of the Diego products to be released this fall will be as good as sales of Dora clothes, DVDs, and toy kitchens, among hundreds of other items. With more than $3.6 billion in sales, Dora products outsell those of any other preschool character.

12   Some people worry that the new shows just bring TV's marketing power to a new and impressionable group of young children. In her magazine article, "Consuming Kids: The Hostile Takeover of Childhood," Susan Linn said watching television is "exactly where the media industry wants (kids)—where they can be marketed to."

13   Still, others are hopeful that television will grow up with today's preschoolers and make prime-time television more diverse. "I think it's catching on," said Christy Glaubke, associate director of Children Now, which studies media and children. "Kids' programming was kind of a testing ground."

---

[3] **census** – an official count of all the people in a country

[4] **Nickelodeon Television** – a cable TV network that broadcasts children's shows

After You Read

Comprehension Check

Circle the letter of the correct answer.

1. What is the main idea of the article?
   a. *Dora the Explorer* is one of the most popular children's shows.
   b. There are more bilingual children's television shows aimed at the Latino audience.
   c. The Disney Channel is planning to feature Latino characters in new shows.

2. What is driving the trend of Latino TV shows?
   a. the growing population of Latino viewers
   b. the growing interest in animation
   c. a bilingual character named Manny Garcia

3. Which is true about children's TV in the past?
   a. There were lots of multicultural shows.
   b. All shows were multicultural.
   c. There were very few multicultural shows.

4. What can you infer from the article?
   a. There is a big market for TV-related products such as dolls, clothes, and toys.
   b. Children don't like toys that are related to TV shows.
   c. There is no relationship between TV and marketing.

5. Which is true about Scholastic Entertainment's show *Maya & Miguel*?
   a. All the characters can speak at least some Spanish.
   b. None of the characters speak Spanish.
   c. The whole show is in Spanish.

6. Which show was the only multicultural children's TV program for many years?
   a. *Jay Jay the Jet Plane*
   b. *Sesame Street*
   c. *Dora the Explorer*

7. According to the article, what are some people worried about?
   a. the amount of violence shown on children's TV
   b. children learning too much Spanish
   c. TV's marketing power aimed at young children

Cartoons are popular with TV viewers everywhere. Here are the favorites in some European countries:
- Spain: *The Jetsons*
- Norway: *Yogi Bear*
- Sweden: *Jonny Quest*
- Finland: *Richie Rich*
- Holland: *Captain Planet*
- U.K., Romania: *The Flintstones*
- France, Poland: *Bugs Bunny and Daffy Duck*

Vocabulary Practice

A Complete the paragraph with the words from the list. Use each word only once.

animated	pilot
characters	prime-time
diversity	spin-off
episode	theme
heroine	

My son is too young for _____ TV, but he watches two

              1.

shows every morning. His favorite show is a(n) _____

                                               2.

program called *The Corner Store*. Some of the _____ in the

                                                  3.

show are African American. Others are white, Latino, and Asian

American. The _____ is a young girl named Sandra. The

                      4.

_____ is growing up in a big city. He also likes to watch the

            5.

_____ called *The Park Across the Street*. It features Sandra's

            6.

cousin Javier. Something funny always happens to them. My son loves

the _____ when Sandra and Javier ride the bus to visit their

            7.

grandmother. Now he is waiting for a new show that's going to start this

fall. He saw the _____ this summer and loved it. The first

            8.

regular show is scheduled for September 10. As a mother, I'm glad that

the new show will also reflect the _____ of our country.

                                            9.

SKILL FOR SUCCESS

Understanding Word Parts: The Prefixes *multi-* and *bi-*
The prefix *multi-* means "many." In this article, you learned the word *multicultural*, which means "having many cultural backgrounds." The prefix *bi-* means "having or using two." In this article, you also learned the word *bilingual*, which means "using two languages."

B Match each word with the correct definition.

	Word		Definition
_____	1. bicycle	**a.**	a person with millions of dollars
_____	2. multicolored	**b.**	involving two groups or two countries
_____	3. bipeds	**c.**	having many uses or abilities
_____	4. multimillionaire	**d.**	animals that walk on two legs
_____	5. multifaceted	**e.**	involving many groups or countries
_____	6. bilateral	**f.**	a two-wheeled vehicle moved by pedals
_____	7. multilateral	**g.**	having many colors
_____	8. bifocals	**h.**	eyeglasses with lenses for seeing close up and seeing far away
_____	9. multimedia	**i.**	using several media such as TV, radio, film

C Complete each sentence with the correct word from Exercise B.

1. I ride my _____ to work even in the rain.

2. Mr. Garcia is very rich. He is a _____.

3. The flag of our organization is _____. It is red, orange, yellow, green, blue, and purple.

4. The agreement was between England and the United States. It was a _____ agreement.

5. There is a _____ exhibit at the art gallery. It includes video, dance, and computer music.

6. My vision is getting worse. Now I have to wear _____.

7. There is a _____ trade agreement among all of the countries of Europe.

8. Humans walk on two feet, and so can many types of birds. Penguins, for example, are _____.

9. She is a _____ performer. She can sing, dance, and play the piano.

Talk It Over

Discuss these questions as a class.

1. Do you think it is important for TV to reflect the demographics of society?
2. Is watching TV an effective way to learn a new language? Why or why not?
3. Do you think children's TV should be commercial-free? Why or why not?

Take a Survey

Find out about people's television-viewing habits. Ask three classmates or other people to answer the questions in the chart. Then discuss your completed surveys in a small group.

Questions	Name: _____	Name: _____	Name: _____
1. How many hours of TV do you usually watch each day?	a. less than 1 b. 1 to 3 c. more than 3	a. less than 1 b. 1 to 3 c. more than 3	a. less than 1 b. 1 to 3 c. more than 3
2. Do you record your favorite shows if you are not at home?	a. always b. sometimes c. never	a. always b. sometimes c. never	a. always b. sometimes c. never
3. What kind of effect do you think TV has on society?	a. a good effect b. no effect c. a bad effect	a. a good effect b. no effect c. a bad effect	a. a good effect b. no effect c. a bad effect
4. Do TV commercials influence what you buy?	a. a lot b. somewhat c. not at all	a. a lot b. somewhat c. not at all	a. a lot b. somewhat c. not at all

Reality TV

Before You Read

A Circle the types of TV programs you like to watch. Then compare answers with a partner.

news and politics	science/technology	crime	cartoons
cooking	home decorating	reality TV	talk shows
gardening	business	music TV	history
game shows	nature/animals	biographies	travel
soap operas	comedies	dramas	movies
medical	shopping	sports	science fiction

B Discuss these questions with a partner.

1. Do you ever watch reality TV shows? If so, which ones?
2. Do you like reality TV? Why or why not?
3. Are reality TV shows popular in your country? If so, which ones are the most popular?

C Learn the meanings of the following words before you read the article.

eliminating (2)   critiques (4)
categories (3)   remodeled (5)
documentary (3)   interfere (6)
contestants (4)   swap (6)

Reality TV

by Daniel Lourie

1   In the past few years, there has been an explosion in a type of television programming called *reality TV*. As its name suggests, reality TV is about real people in real situations. Unlike traditional television shows, reality TV shows are completely unscripted[1]. They allow viewers to watch how real people react in certain situations.

2   Today, about 69 percent of the world's television watching is devoted to reality TV. In fact, some TV stations are completely dedicated to reality TV shows—that's all they show. Whether you are a fan of reality TV or not, it is definitely good business. It seems that lots of people enjoy watching other people's lives. And lots of people like being on television enough to do it for free. By eliminating both writers and actors, the cost of production drops dramatically. Reality shows cost an average of $400,000 per hour to produce as opposed to $2 million an hour for a dramatic series.

3   These days, it seems that people everywhere are discussing what happened on television the night before; and it's not the world news they're talking about. They're talking about what happened on their favorite reality TV show. In schools, offices, health clubs, hair salons, and coffee shops, the hot topic is often reality TV. Although there are hundreds of reality TV programs, most can be grouped into three major categories: contest-based shows, self-improvement shows, and documentary-style shows.

4   Contest-based reality TV shows center around a group of real people competing for a prize based on certain skills. The shows *Survivor* and *American Idol* are examples of contest-based reality TV. Although *Survivor* was not the first reality-based TV show, it is the one that made reality TV a cultural phenomenon. In *Survivor*, the contestants are divided into teams that must work together to survive on an island. In every episode, the teams compete against one another to perform tasks such as building a camp and searching for food. The team that loses has to vote off one member of its group. In the end, there is one survivor left who wins a prize of $1 million. In *American Idol* there are no teams. Instead, individuals compete for a recording contract by singing each week on live television. A panel of judges critiques each contestant's performance. The judges talk about the contestants' strengths and weaknesses. But they do not pick the winner. People in the viewing audience make the decision. They call in to vote for their favorite singer. Each week, the contestant with the fewest votes is eliminated until one final singer remains.

---

[1] **unscripted** – not planned or written down in advance

5   In the category of self-improvement reality shows, the audience watches real people try to improve a specific aspect of their lives. *Extreme Makeover* is an example of a show in this category. *Extreme Makeover* features stories of people who want to look better. Viewers watch as people experience everything from plastic surgery² to changes in their clothing and hairstyles. The show was so popular that a spin-off called *Extreme Makeover: Home Edition* was created. In this program, the house of one lucky family is completely remodeled in just seven days. A team of professional designers and carpenters does the job. *The Biggest Loser* is another example of a self-improvement reality TV series. On *The Biggest Loser*, real people with weight problems work with experienced exercise coaches to lose weight and become healthier people.

6   The third type of reality TV is the documentary-style program. On these shows, the audience and the camera follow regular people going about their daily lives but in an artificially created situation. Unlike other types of reality TV shows, documentary-style programs do not interfere with the people on the show. Examples in this category are *The Real World, Big Brother,* and *Wife Swap. The Real World* focuses on the lives of seven strangers who live in a house together for several months. Cameras record their interpersonal relationships, and viewers just watch. Each season, the show moves to a different city. In *Big Brother*, twelve volunteers spend nine weeks living together in one house, being filmed twenty-four hours a day. Each week, the contestants pick two members of the group who must leave. Viewers make the final decision. *Big Brother* is a hit internationally and has shows in countries all over the world. In *Wife Swap*, two wives change homes and roles for two weeks. Viewers watch how their husbands and children react to the swap.

7   Since reality shows are the most popular and profitable type of television programming, you can expect even more reality TV shows in the future. You can bet that reality TV is here to stay.

---

² **plastic surgery** – medical treatment that changes the way people look, by either repairing injuries or improving their appearance

After You Read

Comprehension Check

A   Read these statements. If a statement is true according to the article, write *T* on the line. If it is false, write *F*.

_____ 1. Reality TV is one of the most popular forms of TV entertainment.

_____ 2. *Survivor* was the first reality show.

_____ 3. *American Idol* is a self-improvement type of reality show.

_____ 4. Reality TV shows cost more to produce than regular shows.

_____ 5. Actors play the parts of real people on reality TV.

_____ 6. More than half of the world's television watching is devoted to reality TV.

_____ 7. Contestants on reality TV programs read from a script.

_____ 8. Some TV stations air only reality shows.

✓ **Using Graphic Organizers: Making a Chart**

B Complete the chart with information from the article.

Type	Definition/Explanation	Examples
1. contest-based		a. b. c.
2.	real people attempt to improve a specific area of their lives	a. b.
3.		a. *The Real World* b. c.

Vocabulary Practice

A Circle the letter of the correct answer.

1. Would you like to be a _____ on a game show?
   a. documentary
   b. category
   c. contestant

2. Did you like the _____ on animal communication?
   a. swap
   b. documentary
   c. category

3. We don't need all these songs on the CD. Let's _____ the last two.
   a. eliminate
   b. interfere
   c. critique

4. The judge will _____ all of the students' paintings.
   a. swap
   b. interfere
   c. critique

5. There are three _____ of children's shows.
   a. categories
   b. swaps
   c. contestants

6. I _____ cars with my brother. I wanted to see how his car drove.
   a. eliminated
   b. swapped
   c. interfered

7. My husband and I want to make our own decisions, but my mother-in-law always _____.
   a. remodels
   b. swaps
   c. interferes

B Cross out the word or phrase in each group that does not belong.

1. producer	contestant	competitor	challenger
2. trade	swap	return	exchange
3. critique	evaluate	criticize	create
4. group	size	category	type
5. remove	eliminate	get rid of	attach
6. alter	change	discuss	remodel

SKILL FOR SUCCESS

Understanding Word Parts: The Suffixes -ship and -ness
Two common suffixes are -ship and -ness. They both mean "state of," but -ship is added to a noun to form a new noun, and -ness is added to an adjective to form a noun. In this chapter, you read the words *relationship* and *weakness*.

C Add the suffix -ship or -ness to each word to make a new word. Use your dictionary to check the spelling and meaning of each new word. Then write a sentence using each word.

   1. companion (noun) *companionship*

   _____

2. tired (adjective) _____

_____

3. ill (adjective) _____

_____

4. kind (adjective) _____

_____

5. lazy (adjective) _____

_____

6. leader (noun) _____

_____

7. member (noun) _____

_____

8. partner (noun) _____

_____

9. selfish (adjective) _____

_____

10. sportsman (noun) _____

_____

D **Answer each question with the correct word from the list of new words in Exercise C.**

1. What is a synonym of *sickness*? _____
2. What quality do you look for in a president of an organization?
   _____
3. What quality does someone who thinks only about himself or herself have? _____
4. What is important in playing competitive sports? _____
5. What is a company that is owned by two people called?
   _____
6. How are all the people who belong to an organization referred to?
   _____
7. What quality is not good for a student to have? _____
8. What is the opposite of *cruelty*? _____
9. What is a synonym for *friendship*? _____
10. What word means "exhaustion"? _____

Talk It Over

Discuss these questions as a class.

1. Why do you think some people like reality TV so much?
2. Do you agree that reality TV is here to stay?
3. Does reality TV present an accurate picture of society?

Discussion

Discuss these questions in a small group.

1. Do you think the invention of the television is as important as the invention of the printing press? Why or why not?
2. Do you think that the news you see on TV is as accurate as the news you read in the paper? Why or why not?
3. What changes in TV programming do you think we can expect in the future?
4. What are the differences between TV in your country and in the United States? What types of programs are most popular in your country?

Just for Fun

Find and circle these twelve words relating to television. The words may be horizontal (↔), vertical (↕), or diagonal (↘). One word has been found for you.

action	commercials	mysteries	sports
cartoons	documentary	news	videotape
comedies	drama	satellite	~~westerns~~

S	Y	Y	O	A	C	T	S	A	T	Y	S	C	T	H
C	L	R	M	V	S	R	E	X	T	E	T	A	C	L
S	J	A	L	L	N	Z	T	Z	I	U	R	R	B	P
R	R	T	I	K	J	P	N	R	F	J	O	T	C	R
D	O	N	Z	C	P	V	E	O	O	X	P	O	Z	O
B	O	E	W	O	R	T	I	D	I	C	S	O	F	A
O	V	M	I	B	S	E	O	D	O	T	C	N	B	Y
N	E	U	C	Y	G	O	M	J	E	V	C	S	J	C
O	H	C	M	M	I	F	F	M	J	O	C	A	O	Y
E	G	O	D	B	O	I	R	H	O	K	T	M	F	R
L	R	D	N	E	W	S	J	R	K	C	E	A	D	N
S	A	T	E	L	L	I	T	E	F	D	F	T	P	Q
E	S	N	Y	R	B	D	H	B	I	U	J	Q	E	E
A	E	W	V	O	N	Q	B	E	K	P	W	F	O	S
A	P	S	N	R	E	T	S	E	W	H	D	A	W	X

Baby TV

This video reports on an increase in television programs designed for children under two years old. Many children watch TV in the United States, but parents do not always feel good about it. Why do you think parents might feel uncomfortable about letting very young children watch TV?

A Study these words and phrases. Then watch the video.

American Academy of Pediatrics   interpret

guinea pigs   under-two set

interaction

B All of the statements below are false. Read the statements and then watch the video again. Rewrite each statement to make it true. Add a detail from the video.

1. Carolyn Mansfield doesn't let her children watch *Sesame Street*.
   Carolyn Mansfield lets her children watch Sesame Street
   because she approves of the content.

2. The American Academy of Pediatrics recommends two hours of TV for children under two.

   _____

3. The recommendation is based on experiments with children.

   _____

4. Most parents know how to interact with their kids when they watch TV.

   _____

5. The best way for children to learn is by watching TV.

   _____

C Discuss these questions with a partner or in a small group.

1. Do you think watching TV is bad for young children? Explain your answer.
2. In your home country, do young children watch a lot of television? Is there a debate about young kids watching TV?

Reader's Journal

Think about the topics and ideas you have read about and discussed in this unit. Pick a topic from the list, one of the discussion questions in the unit, or an idea of your own. Write about it for ten to twenty minutes.

- your favorite TV show
- why TV is good or bad for children
- reality TV
- your favorite TV personality
- the effects of TV on family life, politics, or violence

Vocabulary Self-Test

Complete each sentence with the correct word or phrase.

A animated   brought a halt to   contestant   remodel
   big hit   character   linked

1. _____ shows are especially popular with young children.

2. Lack of money _____ the new highway project.

3. I didn't like that book. I didn't think the main _____ was interesting.

4. In 1869, the transcontinental railroad _____ the eastern and western United States for the first time.

5. Ivan was lucky. His first book was a(n) _____.

6. Our kitchen is twenty-five years old. We want to _____ it.

7. I think it would be fun to be a(n) _____ on a game show.

B categories   documentary   pilot   theme
   craze   heroine   swap   transmitted

1. She became a _____ in our town when she saved the little boy's life.

2. The tennis match will be _____ by satellite.

3. We'll show the _____ program on Tuesday to see how the audience reacts to the _____ of the show.

4. The newest _____ is Sudoku, the logic-based numbers puzzle.

5. I can't see over the woman in front of me. Would you _____ seats with me?

6. Coffee falls into one of three _____: mild, medium, and bold.

7. We watched an excellent _____ about the history of computers. I learned a lot of new information.

C critique   eliminated   interfere   spin-off
   diversity   episode   prime-time   trial and error

1. The _____ of a popular show doesn't usually become a big success.

2. _____ shows are often inappropriate for young children.

3. The final _____ of the show will be on in May.

4. I learned to cook by _____.

5. When the team lost the game today, it was _____ from the tournament.

6. I have to _____ a book for homework tonight.

7. It's better not to _____ in their arguments.

8. The article describes the growing ethnic _____ in our city.

SUPERSTITIONS

A superstition is a belief that certain actions or objects bring good luck or bad luck. Although superstitions are not based on reason or scientific knowledge, we still seem to hold on to some of them. Perhaps this is a way of dealing with things we don't understand. In this unit, you will read about many kinds of superstitions.

Points to Ponder

Read the list of actions that different cultures believe bring good luck or bad luck. Check (✔) whether you think the action brings good luck, brings bad luck, or has no effect. Then compare answers in a small group.

Action	Brings good luck	Brings bad luck	Has no effect
1. breaking a mirror			
2. carrying a rabbit's foot			
3. seeing a black cat			
4. opening an umbrella indoors			
5. crossing your fingers			
6. finding a four-leaf clover			
7. walking under a ladder			
8. knocking on wood			
9. seeing a moving star			
10. spilling salt			
11. washing your hair on the day of a test			
12. finding money on the street			

It's Your Lucky Number!

Before You Read

A Discuss these questions with a partner.

1. What numbers are considered good luck in your country?
2. What numbers are considered bad luck in your country?

✓ **Using Background Knowledge**

B You are going to read about lucky and unlucky numbers. Check (✓) the statements about this topic that you think are true. Then compare answers with a partner.

❑ 1. Different cultures have different ideas about which numbers are lucky and which are unlucky.
❑ 2. Lucky and unlucky numbers are based on science.
❑ 3. Superstitions about numbers are an important part of everyone's everyday life.
❑ 4. People in ancient times thought some numbers brought good luck and others brought bad luck.
❑ 5. All people agree that the number 13 brings bad luck.

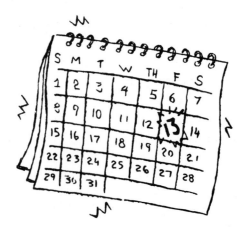

C Learn the meanings of the following words before you read the article.

notion (1)   rearranging (5)
skip (2)   acquire (7)
feast (3)   security (9)
banned (4)

It's Your Lucky Number!

1   Do you think some numbers are lucky and others are unlucky? Most cultures have good luck and bad luck numbers. The notion that numbers can bring good luck or bad luck is a superstition.

Unlucky Numbers

2   The number 13 is considered unlucky by superstitious people in North and South America and in Europe. It is such a strong superstition that many airlines do not have a Flight 13. Lots of planes don't have a Row 13, either. The same is true for tall buildings. If you are in an elevator, you may notice that there is no button for the 13th floor. The buttons go from 12 to 14 and skip 13. Some people avoid starting trips or other activities on the 13th day of a month. The English language even has a word for the fear of the number 13. It's *triskaidekaphobia*. Are you triskaidekaphobic?

3   We do not know how the number 13 came to be considered unlucky. There are several theories. One is that it comes from the ancient Roman belief that 13 was a sign of death and destruction. Other people think it all started with an old Viking[1] story about a feast for twelve gods. The evil god, Loki, was not invited, but he came anyway. That made thirteen guests. According to the story, Loki killed one of the other gods. Since then, the number 13 has been considered bad luck. Some superstitious people believe it is unlucky for thirteen to eat dinner together. One of them will die within a year. Another story comes from Christianity. There were thirteen people at the last supper of Jesus Christ. The next day, he was killed.

4   While 13 is considered unlucky in the West, in many Asian countries, such as China, Japan, and Korea, the number 4 is an unlucky number. That's because the word for *four* sounds like the word for *death*. In Asia, many hotels have no 4th floor. In Seoul's Inchon Airport, there are no gates 4 or 44. And you won't find the 4th or 14th floors in many Chinese buildings. Chinese people often avoid using 4 in their phone numbers, home addresses, and license plates. Two Chinese cities even banned the numeral 4 from license plates. In all of these countries, it's a bad idea to give gifts in sets of four.

5   The numbers 13 and 4 are not the only

---

[1] **Viking** – refers to the Scandinavians who invaded Europe from the eighth to the eleventh centuries

ones associated with bad luck. For example, 17 is considered unlucky in Italy because rearranging the letters in the Roman numerals for 17 could spell VIXI which means "I lived" (or "I'm dead") in Latin. The number 9 can also bring bad luck in some places. *Nine* is pronounced as "*ku*" in Japanese, which is similar to the word *pain*. Hospitals usually don't have 9th floors in Japan.

Lucky Numbers

6   Just as some numbers are supposed to be bad luck, there are some numbers that are considered lucky. For example, 7 is considered a lucky number by some superstitious people in Western cultures. Why is 7 lucky? No one knows for sure where the idea came from, but there are many special 7s: seven days of the week, seven Wonders of the World, seven colors of the spectrum, and so on.

7   In China, many people believe that 8 is a very lucky number. Why? The word for *eight* sounds like the word for *to acquire wealth* or *to become rich*. People pay extra fees to get 8s in their phone numbers, home addresses, and license plate numbers. In Hong Kong, it can cost millions of dollars to get a numeral 8 on your license plate. The number 8 is so lucky that the mayor of Beijing announced that the 2008 Olympic Games in Beijing would begin at 8:00 p.m. on August 8!

8   Three is also a lucky number in China because the word for *three* sounds like the word for *life*. A man in Beijing paid $215,000 to get the luckiest cell phone number: 133-3333-3333.

9   In fact, there is nothing lucky or unlucky about any number. Still, many people believe that a number can bring good or bad luck. Most of us have fears that make us feel insecure. Superstitions help us overcome these fears by providing security. With all the uncertainty in the world, one thing is certain: None of us knows what tomorrow will bring.

After You Read

Comprehension Check

✓ **Making Inferences**

A Write the number of the paragraph that answers each question.

1. Why do some people believe that the number 8 is lucky? _____

2. Where is the number 4 considered unlucky? _____

3. What theories are there about how the number 13 came to be considered unlucky? _____

4. What are some examples of superstitions associated with the number 13? _____

5. What numbers, besides 13 and 4, are considered unlucky in some cultures? _____

B Check (✔) the statements that are inferences based on information in the article.

☐ 1. Numbers were important in some ancient societies.
☐ 2. There are only three theories about how the number 13 came to be considered unlucky.
☐ 3. Starting a new job on the 13th day of the month could be a problem for some people who are superstitious.
☐ 4. Superstitions are based on scientific facts.
☐ 5. Some superstitious people would not invite thirteen people to a dinner party.
☐ 6. Many Chinese would be happy to have the number 8 in their phone number.
☐ 7. There is scientific proof that the number 7 has special powers.

✓ **Scanning**

C Scan the article for the answer to each question. Work as quickly as possible.

1. What does the word *triskaidekaphobia* mean? _____
2. Where is 4 an unlucky number? _____
3. What do the Roman numerals VIXI mean? _____
4. What does the word for the number 8 sound like in Chinese?
   _____
5. On what date will the 2008 Olympic Games in Beijing begin?
   _____

Vocabulary Practice

A Complete each sentence with the correct word(s).

acquired	rearrange
banned	security
feast	skip
notion	

1. I'll _____ my schedule so I can have lunch with you on Friday at noon. But that means I'll have to _____ a meeting at work.

2. Guns, knives, cigarette lighters, and scissors are just a few of the things that are _____ on planes. This should provide more _____ to passengers.

3. After years of hard work as a collector, Mr. Lee _____ both wealth and many valuable stamps.

4. In many stories, a great _____ is given to honor the birth of a prince.

5. The _____ that 13 is an unlucky number is probably thousands of years old.

B Circle the letter of the correct answer.

1. If you <u>skipped</u> your friend's graduation party, you _____.
   a. went to it   **b.** did not go to it

2. If you have job <u>security</u>, you _____.
   a. are afraid of losing your job   **b.** aren't worried about losing your job

3. When a museum <u>acquires</u> some new paintings, it _____.
   a. gives them away   **b.** gets them from somewhere

4. At a <u>feast</u>, you would have _____.
   a. interesting books and movies **b.** lots of good food

5. If you accept the <u>notion</u> that some numbers bring bad luck, you _____.
   a. believe it   **b.** don't believe it

6. If smoking is <u>banned</u> in an airport, you _____.
   a. can smoke there   **b.** cannot smoke there

7. If you <u>rearrange</u> the furniture in your living room, the room _____.
   a. looks different   **b.** looks the same

C Cross out the word or phrase in each group that does not belong.

1. idea	notion	belief	fact
2. skip	omit	add	leave out
3. prohibit	ban	allow	forbid
4. meal	feast	banquet	exercise
5. security	concern	safety	protection
6. gain	acquire	lose	get

✓ Learning Homonyms

D Read these sentences. Write the meaning and part of speech of each underlined word. You may need to use your dictionary.

1. **a.** There is no <u>Row</u> 13 on this plane.
   Meaning: _____
   Part of speech: _____
   b. My arms are tired from <u>rowing</u> the boat.
   Meaning: _____
   Part of speech: _____

2. **a.** The floor numbers <u>skip</u> 13. They go from 12 to 14.
   Meaning: _____
   Part of speech: _____
   b. My daughter learned to <u>skip</u> when she was three.
   Meaning: _____
   Part of speech: _____

3. **a.** Please push the <u>button</u> for the 12th floor.
   Meaning: _____
   Part of speech: _____
   b. You need to <u>button</u> your coat; it's windy outside.
   Meaning: _____
   Part of speech: _____

4. **a.** The little boy <u>tripped</u> when he walked into the room.
   Meaning: _____
   Part of speech: _____
   b. How was your <u>trip</u> to New York?
   Meaning: _____
   Part of speech: _____

5. **a.** There's a <u>sign</u> for a gas station. We'd better stop here.
   Meaning: _____
   Part of speech: _____
   b. Did you <u>sign</u> the lease for your new apartment yet?
   Meaning: _____
   Part of speech: _____

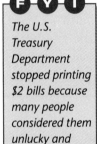

The U.S. Treasury Department stopped printing $2 bills because many people considered them unlucky and refused to use them.

✓ **Using Graphic Organizers: Making a Chart**
Read the paragraph and complete the chart that follows with information from the paragraph.

Food and Superstitions

Many societies around the world have superstitions connected with food. The ancient Egyptians, for example, thought onions kept evil spirits away. When they took an oath (made a promise), they placed one hand on an onion. The custom of throwing rice at weddings goes back to the time in Europe when people thought rice, a symbol of health and prosperity, would calm evil spirits so they would not bother the wedding couple. In Hungary, superstitious people throw salt on the door of a new house to protect them from evil spirits. Superstitious Europeans used to put mustard seeds on the roof of their homes to keep vampires away. In Japan, during the festival of Setsuben, people put beans in dark corners and entrances of the home to drive out evil spirits. For many years, Europeans have used garlic as a charm against evil spirits. Some wore garlic around their necks. Others placed garlic over their doors for protection. ■

Food	Superstition	Place of Origin	Effect
1. *onion*	*placing a hand on an onion while taking an oath*	*Egypt*	*kept evil spirits away*
2.			
3.			
4.			
5.			
6.			

Talk It Over

Discuss these questions as a class.

1. Do you have a lucky number? If so, what is it? How did you choose it? When do you use your lucky number?
2. What are some food superstitions in your country? Do you know where they came from?

Superstitious Athletes

Before You Read

A Discuss these questions with a partner.

1. What superstitions do you know that relate to sports?
2. Are there any famous athletes in your country who are known for their superstitions?
3. Why do you think so many athletes are superstitious?

✓ **Skimming for the Main Idea**

B Skim the article one time. Then choose the statement you think describes the main idea.

1. Many athletes are superstitious.
2. Some athletes dress the same way every day.
3. Some sports superstitions are strange.

C Learn the meanings of the following words and phrases before you read the article.

passed up (2)   quirk (5)
illusion (3)   hung up on (5)
rituals (3)   weird (8)
stick to (3)

Superstitious Athletes

by Walter Roessing

1 Did you know that golfer Tiger Woods always wears a red shirt on the last day of a tournament? Or that basketball superstar Michael Jordan always wore his blue University of North Carolina shorts under his Chicago Bulls uniform? Racecar driver Mario Andretti wouldn't enter a car from the right side. Are you surprised that hockey star and coach Wayne Gretzky won't get his hair cut when his team plays away games because they lost one night after he got a haircut? All of these athletes have one thing in common: They are all superstitious.

2 "Athletes are more superstitious than most people," says Oakland Raiders football player Ronnie Lott. He always wears his lucky swim shorts under his uniform. The one time he forgot to wear his lucky shorts for a game, he hurt his shoulder. "Athletes do all kinds of crazy things to guarantee victory or make sure they won't get hurt." Lott has food superstitions, too. He always eats a hamburger the night before a game. Several years ago, his team was playing an away game on Thanksgiving Day. The night before, Lott passed up a turkey dinner with his teammates to dine alone at Wendy's.

3 Thomas Tutko is a sports psychologist. He says, "Whatever the superstitions, they help athletes and coaches relax." They give players the illusion of control. Superstitious beliefs often involve rituals about uniforms, food, or numbers. Many athletes think if they stick to a routine, it will help them win. Tutko recalls working with San Jose-area high school basketball players who believed they were winning because of their white socks. "They refused to wash their socks all season," Tutko says.

4 Athletes have been known to wear the same uniforms without washing them until their team loses. Other athletes always get dressed in a specific sequence. They say these rituals bring them good luck. The famous boxer Joe Louis believed that he would lose a fight if his right glove was put on before the left one. Baseball pitcher Turk Wendell brushed his teeth and ate licorice candy between every inning[1]. Los Angeles Dodgers player Nomar Garciaparra gets dressed the same way every day. He also makes sure to step on each step of the dugout with both feet, and he taps his toes when it is his turn to bat.

5 Former baseball player Wade Boggs is almost as famous for his superstitions as he is for his athletic ability. He ate chicken before every game. That quirk started when Boggs was playing in the minor leagues[2]. "On the days when I ate chicken, I always got two hits," he says. Boggs was hung up on the numbers 7 and 17, too. Before a night game, he always ran in the outfield at exactly 7:17 P.M.

6 Boggs isn't the only athlete with superstitions about numbers. Mario

---

[1] **inning** – one of the nine playing periods in the game of baseball

[2] **minor leagues** – the groups of teams that form the lower levels of American professional baseball

Andretti wouldn't stay in a hotel room with the numeral 13. Baltimore Orioles pitcher Jose Mercedes had a problem with the number 3. He wouldn't pitch in the third game of a season.

7 Tony La Russa is the manager of the St. Louis Cardinals baseball team. He has an unusual superstition involving writing: He prints the names of the players' batting order for every game until they lose. Then he switches to cursive writing. When St. Louis loses again, he goes back to printing.

8 Some rituals seem very weird. Here's an example: Mark van Eeghen played football for the Oakland Raiders. Before each game, he climbed on top of the television set in his hotel room and jumped to the bed. He felt that this would protect him from getting hurt on the field. But one time, he missed the bed and fell. His injury forced him to miss a game.

9 It seems some athletes will do anything for good luck! ■

After You Read

Comprehension Check

A Write the answer to each question. Then compare answers with a partner.

1. Why do some athletes believe in superstitions?

_____

2. According to sports psychologist Thomas Tutko, what is the benefit of superstitions?

_____

3. What three areas do superstitious beliefs often involve?

_____

✓ **Using Graphic Organizers: Making a Chart**

B Complete the chart with information from the article.

Name of Athlete	Sport	Superstitions
1. Tiger Woods	*golf*	*wears a red shirt on the last day of a tournament*
2.	basketball	
3. Mario Andretti		
4.		won't get his hair cut when his team plays away games
5. Ronnie Lott		
6.	boxing	
7. Turk Wendell		
8.		gets dressed the same way; steps on each step of the dugout with both feet, and taps his toes when it's his turn to bat
9.	baseball	
10.		wouldn't pitch in the third game of a season
11. Tony La Russa		
12.	football	

✓ **Identifying Facts and Opinions**

C Decide if each statement is a fact or an opinion. Check (✓) the correct box.

	Fact	Opinion
1. Mario Andretti wouldn't enter a car from the right side.		
2. Athletes do all kinds of crazy things to guarantee victory or make sure they won't get hurt.		
3. Thomas Tutko is a sports psychologist.		
4. Former baseball player Wade Boggs is almost as famous for his superstitions as he is for his athletic ability.		
5. Before a night game, Boggs always ran in the outfield at exactly 7:17 P.M.		
6. Some rituals seem very weird.		
7. Mark van Eeghen played football for the Oakland Raiders.		
8. It seems some athletes will do anything for good luck!		

Vocabulary Practice

A Match each word or phrase with the correct definition.

Word or Phrase	Definition
_____ 1. pass up	**a.** strange
_____ 2. illusion	**b.** to follow
_____ 3. quirk	**c.** something that is not what it seems to be
_____ 4. stick to	**d.** a set of actions always done in the same way
_____ 5. ritual	**e.** worried about something
_____ 6. hung up on	**f.** an unusual habit
_____ 7. weird	**g.** to decide not to take advantage of an opportunity

B Complete each sentence with the correct word or phrase from Exercise A.

1. Athletes like superstitions because they give them the _____ of control.

2. Most of us have a _____ or two that may seem odd.

3. Why did you _____ the chance to go to the concert?

4. What is that strange noise coming from the hall? It sounds really _____.

5. Don is _____ getting the highest grades in the class.

6. My daughter has a nightly _____. She always takes a bath, has a glass of milk, and reads a chapter in a book.

7. Please _____ the schedule I wrote on the blackboard.

✓ **Learning Synonyms and Antonyms**

C For each pair of words, circle *S* if they are synonyms or *A* if they are antonyms.

1. stick to	follow	*S*	*A*
2. illusion	reality	*S*	*A*
3. pass up	accept	*S*	*A*
4. quirk	oddity	*S*	*A*
5. routine	ritual	*S*	*A*
6. weird	normal	*S*	*A*
7. concerned about	hung up on	*S*	*A*

Athletes aren't the only group of superstitious people. Actors are often superstitious, too. Have you ever heard of any of the following superstitions about the theater? Use the Internet or library to find out which actions are supposed to bring good luck to actors and which are supposed to bring bad luck. Write *good luck* or *bad luck* on the lines.

1. wishing an actor "Good luck!" before a performance _____*bad luck*_____
2. receiving a bouquet of flowers before the play begins _____
3. seeing a cat in the theater _____
4. wearing the color blue _____
5. leaving one light burning in the theater when no one is there

   _____
6. using real mirrors or real jewelry on stage _____
7. pinching an actor or actress before he or she goes on the stage for the first time _____
8. speaking the last line of the play during rehearsals _____

Discuss these questions as a class.

1. Are you superstitious? If so, what are your superstitions?
2. Do you have any rituals? If so, what are they?
3. Do you find that your rituals help you? If so, how?

UNIT 6

CHAPTER 3

It's Jinxed!

Before You Read

A Discuss these questions with a partner.

1. Some people believe that certain objects bring good luck and others bring bad luck. Do you think this is true?
2. A four-leaf clover is often considered lucky in some cultures. What are some things that are considered lucky in your culture? Do you have any good-luck charms?

✔ **Using Background Information**

B You are going to read an article about the Hope Diamond and the Pharaoh's Curse. Work with a partner to answer these questions.

1. Look at the photo of the Hope Diamond in the article. Have you ever heard of the Hope Diamond? If so, what do you know about it?
2. Do you know about the curse of the tomb of King Tutankhamen in Egypt? If so, what do you know about it?

C Learn the meanings of the following words before you read the article.

reputation (1)   blamed (8)

misfortune (2)   eager (9)

legend (2)   hoaxes (9)

tragedies (4)

It's Jinxed!

1 Some people believe that certain objects are supposed to bring good luck. For example, many Chinese people believe objects made of jade bring good luck. On the other hand, certain objects and even certain places have a reputation of being jinxed, that is, of bringing bad luck. The Hope Diamond and the tomb of ancient Egyptian pharaoh Tutankhamen are both said to be jinxed.

The Hope Diamond

2 The Hope Diamond, one of the world's greatest gems, supposedly brings misfortune to its owners. For years, people have been fascinated by its perfect quality, large size, and rare blue color, which make it unique as well as beautiful. But according to an old legend, this precious stone is jinxed.

The Hope Diamond is said to bring bad luck to its owners.

3 How did the legend of the curse begin? Superstitions about the Hope Diamond go back to 1642 when, according to the legend, it was stolen from the forehead of the statue of a goddess in India. According to the legend, anyone who owned or even touched the diamond would be cursed with bad luck or death. Over the years, the Hope Diamond has had many famous owners, including King Louis XVI and Queen Marie Antoinette. Some people believe the royal couple had their heads cut off during the French Revolution because of the blue diamond's curse.

4 The diamond is named after another one of its owners, Henry Philip Hope, who bought it in the middle of the nineteenth century. The legend says that the diamond brought bad luck to several generations of the Hope family, and eventually the wealthy Hope family lost all their money. Superstitious people believed all of these tragedies were a result of the curse.

5 After the Hope family lost ownership of the diamond, it changed hands[1] several times. It belonged to a New York gem dealer, a Turkish diplomat, a French diamond expert, and French jeweler Pierre Cartier. All the while, tales of its curse continued. In 1911, Cartier sold it to a woman named Evalyn Walsh McLean. Mrs. McLean was part of high society in Washington, D.C., but her life was filled with tragedy. Her son was hit by a car and died. Her husband got into political trouble and divorced her. Her daughter committed suicide. Although McLean didn't believe the diamond was jinxed, her misfortunes helped reinforce the diamond's bad reputation.

6 Today, the Hope Diamond is on display in the Smithsonian Institution in Washington, D.C. Its reputation for bad luck does not keep thousands of visitors from flocking to see it every year.

[1] **change hands** – to become someone else's property

The Pharaoh's Curse

7   Places as well as objects can be jinxed. For example, consider the story of the "Pharaoh's Curse." The rulers, or kings, of ancient Egypt were called pharaohs. The Pharaoh's Curse refers to an old superstition that anyone who disturbs the mummy of an ancient Egyptian pharaoh will be cursed and die. Although

The discovery of King Tutankhamen's tomb started talk of a mummy curse.

that superstition may sound strange today, people were more superstitious in the past.

8   In 1922, a team of archaeologists headed by Howard Carter and Lord Carnarvon made a spectacular discovery. They uncovered the tomb of the ancient Egyptian pharaoh Tutankhamen. The news made headlines all over the world. Shortly after the tomb was opened, three people connected with the expedition died. This coincidence caused a flood of stories that the tomb was cursed. In truth, all three had died of different causes, and their deaths were natural. Then, when Lord Carnarvon died a few weeks later, his death was immediately blamed on the Pharaoh's Curse, too. The story of the Pharaoh's Curse was kept alive for years in newspapers and magazines.

9   The curse was mysterious, but it was also a fraud. It was invented by eager reporters who wanted to give their readers exciting stories. They knew stories of the curse would sell more newspapers and magazines. There was even a story that the words "Death to those who enter this tomb" were carved above the tomb door. But this inscription never existed. Lord Carnarvon did not die from the curse. In fact, he probably died from an infected mosquito bite. Reporters never bothered to inform readers that dozens of others connected with the expedition lived long and successful lives after entering the tomb. Like many members of the expedition, Howard Carter lived a normal life span. He died in 1939 at the age of sixty-six. In the end, the curse of the mummy proved to be one of the biggest hoaxes in the history of superstition. ■

After You Read

Comprehension Check

A Read these statements. If a statement is true according to the article, write *T* on the line. If it is false, write *F*.

_____ 1. Since the Hope Diamond is supposed to be jinxed, few people want to get near it.

_____ 2. Both places and objects can have reputations for being jinxed.

_____ 3. When the tomb of Pharaoh Tutankhamen was discovered, there were articles about it in newspapers all over the world.

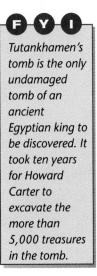

FYI

Tutankhamen's tomb is the only undamaged tomb of an ancient Egyptian king to be discovered. It took ten years for Howard Carter to excavate the more than 5,000 treasures in the tomb.

_____ 4. According to the legend, three people died from the curse right after the tomb was opened.

_____ 5. The words "Death to those who enter this tomb" are written above the door of Tutankhamen's tomb.

_____ 6. The Pharaoh's Curse is one of the biggest hoaxes in the history of superstitions.

_____ 7. Howard Carter died soon after the discovery of the tomb.

_____ 8. Reporters helped to spread the story of the curse of the pharaoh's tomb.

SKILL FOR SUCCESS

Summarizing

Summarizing is a strategy that helps you understand what you read. When you summarize, you write the author's main ideas in your own words. Summarizing will also help you remember what you read.

B Complete the summary with information from the article.

Some people believe that certain _____ and
                                              1.
_____ can bring _____. One example
        2.   3.
of an object that has a reputation of bringing bad luck is

_____. According to _____,
                4.   5.
whoever owns _____. An example
                            6.
of a place that is supposed to be cursed is

_____. Stories about this place say that
                7.
many people who _____.
                                8.

Vocabulary Practice

A Circle the letter of the correct answer.

1. Which is an example of a <u>hoax</u>?
   a. Someone yells, "Fire!" in a theater, and everyone runs out, but there really was no fire.
   b. Someone pulls the fire alarm because there is a fire in the building.

2. <u>Legends</u> are _____ stories.
   a. always true   b. often untrue

Chapter 3   **151**

3. Which is an example of a <u>tragedy</u>?
　　a. An earthquake destroyed　**b.** Your team lost the
　　　a whole town.　　　　　　　　soccer game.

4. If a teacher has a good <u>reputation</u>, people _____.
　　a. think well of him or her　**b.** think badly of him or her

5. If a person is <u>eager</u> to meet you, he _____.
　　a. wants to meet you　　　**b.** doesn't care about meeting you

6. If something brings you <u>misfortune</u>, you are _____.
　　a. happy about it　　　　**b.** unhappy about it

7. If you <u>blame</u> your brother for breaking your computer, you
　　_____.
　　a. aren't sure who broke it　**b.** think your brother broke it

✓ **Using Context Clues**
B **Use context clues to write a definition or synonym for each underlined word. Then compare definitions with a partner.**

1. Certain objects and even certain places have a reputation of being <u>jinxed</u>, that is, of bringing bad luck.

　　_____

2. Its reputation for bad luck does not keep thousands of visitors from <u>flocking</u> to see it every year.

　　_____

3. There was even a story that the words "Death to those who enter this tomb" were carved above the tomb door. But this <u>inscription</u> never existed.

　　_____

4. The curse was mysterious, but it was also a <u>fraud</u>. It was invented by eager reporters who wanted to give their readers exciting stories.

　　_____

5. The rulers, or kings, of ancient Egypt were called <u>pharaohs</u>.

　　_____

6. Shortly after the tomb was opened, three people connected with the expedition died. This <u>coincidence</u> caused a flood of stories that the tomb was cursed.

　　_____

✓ **Learning Synonyms and Antonyms**

C For each pair of words, circle *S* if they are synonyms or *A* if they are antonyms.

1. fraud	hoax	*S*	*A*
2. king	pharaoh	*S*	*A*
3. misfortune	luck	*S*	*A*
4. jinxed	cursed	*S*	*A*
5. eager	unenthusiastic	*S*	*A*
6. legend	tale	*S*	*A*

Write a Newspaper Story

Imagine that you are a reporter in 1923. Write a story for your newspaper. Report on the curses associated with the discovery of the pharaoh Tutankhamen's tomb. Be sure to include a headline that will catch your readers' attention.

_____

_____

_____

_____

_____

_____

_____

Tie It All Together

Discussion

Discuss these questions in a small group.

1. Why do you think people have believed in superstitions for thousands of years?
2. Do you think that there is truth behind superstitions?
3. An ancient Chinese curse says, "May your every wish be granted." How could having *all* your wishes come true be bad?

Just for Fun

Answer each item in the spaces provided. The last letter of an answer will always be the first letter of the next answer.

1. What place is thought to be jinxed?
   _T_ _u_ _t_ _a_ _n_ _k_ _h_ _a_ _m_ _e_ _n_'s
   _t_ _o_ _m_ _b_

2. What brings seven years of bad luck?
   _b_ _r_ _e_ _a_ _k_ _i_ _n_ _g_ a _m_ _i_ _r_ _r_ _o_ _r_

3. What team did Mark van Eeghen play for?
   ___ ___ ___ ___ ___ ___ ___ ___

4. What number means good luck in many cultures?
   ___ ___ ___ ___ ___

5. What kind of life span did Howard Carter live?
   ___ ___ ___ ___ ___ ___

6. Who is the manager of the St. Louis Cardinals?
   ___ ___ ___ ___ ___ ___ ___

7. Where is the number 4 unlucky?
   ___ ___ ___ ___

8. What do you use to hit a baseball?
   ___ ___ ___ ___

9. What's the day after today?
   ___ ___ ___ ___ ___ ___ ___ ___

10. In which city is the Hope Diamond now?
    ___ ___ ___ ___ ___ ___ ___ ___ ___ ___ ___

Video Activity

The Pharaoh's Curse

This video explores the curse of King Tutankhamen's tomb. As you think about your reading in this unit, why do you think so many people believed that this tomb was cursed? What about the story made people superstitious?

A note about the baseball references at the beginning of the video: Many fans of the Chicago Cubs and the Boston Red Sox (both are baseball teams) are superstitious. They thought the teams were cursed. Neither team had won the World Series for many years—since the early 1900s. The Red Sox's curse was finally broken when they won the World Series in 2004: after 86 years!

A Study these words and phrases. Then watch the video.

attributed	microbes
casket	put into context
fueling	riddle
got fed up	

B Read the partial sentences in the left and right columns and then watch the video again. Match the first part of each sentence in the left column with the second part of the sentence in the right column.

_____ 1. The Pyramids

     a. are a likely explanation for the deaths that occurred when the tomb was opened.

_____ 2. Howard Carter

     b. is one of the seven wonders of the world.

_____ 3. Germs and other natural causes

     c. is a 4,500-year-old riddle.

_____ 4. The Great Pyramid in Giza

     d. were built more than 4,000 years ago.

_____ 5. The secret of the Sphinx

     e. discovered and opened King Tutankhamen's tomb in 1922.

C Discuss these questions with a partner or in a small group.

Why do you think many people continue to believe in curses even after scientific explanations are given? Why is it hard to overcome a superstition?

Reader's Journal

Think about the topics and ideas you have read about and discussed in this unit. Pick a topic from the list, one of the discussion questions in the unit, or an idea of your own. Write about it for ten to twenty minutes.

- some superstitions you have
- why people believe in superstitions
- why superstitions are silly
- superstitions in your country

Complete each sentence with the correct word or phrase.

A acquired   hung up on   misfortune   stick to
    hoax   legend   security

1. We had the _____ of being on the road when the snowstorm hit.

2. It will be much easier if we all _____ the schedule.

3. Allow plenty of time to go through the _____ check at the airport.

4. Think about how much English you have _____ in the last month.

5. Elvis Presley is a rock and roll _____.

6. It's not always easy to determine if something is real or a(n) _____.

7. Yasumasa is really _____ winning the pie-eating contest. It's all he thinks about.

B eager   illusion   quirks   weird
    feast   pass up   rituals

1. The magician seemed to make a hat disappear. But it was just a(n) _____.

2. It's _____, but I don't like chocolate. It's one of my _____.

3. Jason decided to _____ the opportunity to work with his father-in-law.

4. Magdalena works really hard because she is _____ for success.

5. There will be lots of excellent food at our wedding. It will be a real _____.

6. I love all the _____ our family has for making food for our Thanksgiving dinner.

C banned   notion   reputation   tragedy
   blamed   rearranged   skipping

1. Where do you think she got the silly _____ that she could lose weight by _____ meals?

2. Bahar has a _____ for honesty. Everyone trusts her.

3. We _____ the furniture in our living room last night.

4. The city _____ smoking in public places in 1995.

5. The fire department _____ a burning cigarette for the fire in her bedroom.

6. The flood caused millions of dollars of destruction. It was the worst _____ we've had in years.

OUR FRAGILE PLANET

People everywhere are becoming more aware of their responsibility for the health of our planet. As you read this unit, think about the effects humans have on nature and the environment.

Points to Ponder

Think about these questions and discuss them in a small group.

1. People all over the world celebrate World Earth Day on April 22. The purpose is to remember that the Earth is precious and we need to take care of it. Look at the picture of the Chinese World Earth Day stamp. Describe the stamp.

2. How have people helped and hurt our planet?

3. Do you do anything personally to help protect our planet? If so, what?

One Family with the Earth

Before You Read

A Discuss these questions with a partner.

1. What do you think the title, "One Family with the Earth," means?
2. Chief Seattle was a Native American who gave a famous speech to the U.S. Congress. Read the excerpt from his speech. Why do you think he calls the flowers "our sisters" and the deer, horse, and eagle "our brothers"?

> We are part of the Earth, and it is part of us. The perfumed flowers are our sisters; the deer, the horse, the great eagle, these are our brothers. The rocky crests, the flowers in the meadows, the body heat of the pony, and man—all belong to the same family.
>
> Chief Seattle of the Suquamish, 1854

✓ **Using Background Knowledge**

B You are going to read an interview with a Native American about the relationship between humans and nature. Check (✓) the statements about this topic that you think are true.

☐ 1. Everyone has the same ideas about how to live with nature.
☐ 2. Some people believe we can own land.
☐ 3. Some people believe that land belongs to everyone, that it cannot be bought or sold.
☐ 4. Many kinds of animals are disappearing from the Earth.
☐ 5. It is important for people to take care of the Earth.
☐ 6. We need to teach our children new values about what is right and wrong.
☐ 7. Our possessions are more important than the Earth and our fellow creatures.

C Learn the meanings of the following words and phrase before you read the article.

sacred (3)   ramifications (5)   horrify (11)
conservation (4)   conquest (8)   species (11)
conscious (5)   fancy (11)   stick up for (15)

One Family with the Earth

1   Native people think about the preservation of the Earth, plants, and animals in a special way. In this interview, you will read about the views of a Native American named Manitonquat (Medicine Man). Manitonquat is a member of the Wampanoag Nation of Massachusetts. He is a writer, storyteller, educator, and ceremonial medicine man[1]. He says that native people around the world share the attitude that the Earth is spiritually alive and that people may live with it but do not own it.

2 **Reporter:** How do native people view the Earth?

3 **Manitonquat:** As a native, I have been taught that we must be the caretakers of the Earth. We call the Earth our mother because taking care of it is a primary responsibility, like caring for our parents and our children. Our people are taught to act and walk lightly upon this Earth in a sacred manner, making every step upon the Earth Mother as a prayer so that seven generations yet to come may follow our paths in safety.

4 **Reporter:** Did native people of America practice any conservation measures before other settlers came?

5 **Manitonquat:** Native people were environmentally conscious because they lived close to the environment. Others don't realize how much care they took in the woods. In everything they did, they were conscious of the fact that if you disturb something, it will have ramifications through the whole web of life. So they were very careful about disturbing anything.

6   Human beings are very intelligent and take good care of themselves. But what happened in civilization is that human beings' intelligence went off in other

[1] **medicine man** – someone who is believed to have special powers to heal people

directions and developed technology, arts, and such things to the point where they began to be removed from their natural environment. When you build a city around you, the younger generations begin to think that milk comes from a carton and not from an animal.

7 **Reporter:** How did Native Americans view the arrival of European settlers?

8 **Manitonquat:** When Europeans first came, the Native Americans welcomed them and thought they would act like human beings in the natives' understanding of how human beings are supposed to relate to the Earth. But the Europeans came here with conquest in mind. They took what land they could take, bought what they could buy, and stole and fought for the rest. Suddenly we discovered that they thought we were subjects of their kings and that we had given them this land forever. Nobody owns land. You can use it, have your animals on it, hunt, and so forth, but the land is here forever. We are part of it.

9 **Reporter:** What needs to be done for the Earth?

10 **Manitonquat:** We need to think about a whole new set of values to give to our kids. A lot of native people like myself go to schools whenever we get a chance. We take the kids out into the woods and say, "Here, these are your relatives. Sit with this tree. Talk to this tree. Listen to this tree. Hug this tree. This is your friend."

11 The Earth and our fellow creatures are more valuable than all the fancy things we have. It should horrify all human beings that we are losing whole species of animals and birds. There are very few free-flying California condors left in California, and several hundred beluga whales in the St. Lawrence River are dying of cancer from industrial wastes.

12 **Reporter:** What do we need to do to be friends with the Earth?

13 **Manitonquat:** One thing people can do is to get closer to the Earth. If you go camping or on a picnic, take the time to look at what's around, and talk about the plants, birds, and whatever comes by. When I was a kid, my grandfather took me out. We had names for all the animals, and he told me about the plants. He told me to talk to them and to listen to them. He said there were stones that had spirits. You could feel the spirit and know that it had been there for a long time and had seen a lot of things; you could get a lot of knowledge from that stone.

14 **Reporter:** What does it mean to be friends with the Earth?

15 **Manitonquat:** When you're somebody's friend, you don't let anybody hurt him, you stick up for him. It makes you feel good to be with him. Everything in the universe is important; everything has its purpose and its reason. We are here as part of the Earth. It was put here for more than just our pleasure. It must support many things.

16 Often I say to children that if you are the elder brother or sister, you have to speak for the little baby who cannot talk. You speak for the grass because it's not able to talk. If you were a blade of grass, what would you say? If you were a little squirrel, what would you say? If you were the Mother Earth herself, what would you say about what's happening to you? ∎

After You Read

✓ **Making Inferences**

Read the statements. Make inferences about which statements you think Manitonquat would agree with and which ones you think he would not agree with. Check (✔) *Yes* or *No*.

	Yes	No
1. Taking care of the Earth should be one of humanity's most important responsibilities.		
2. Parents and children have a responsibility to each other.		
3. Land should belong to whoever is willing to fight the hardest for it or pay the most money for it.		
4. We should care about the Earth and all living plants and animals more than we care about expensive things we can buy.		
5. We don't need to worry too much about animals that are dying out. They will take care of themselves.		
6. It is only possible to communicate with and learn from living creatures.		
7. Only some things in the world are important. We can ignore other things.		
8. The European settlers' view of humans' relationship with the Earth surprised the Native Americans.		
9. Children who live in cities need to have experiences that bring them closer to nature.		

A Choose the correct definition or synonym for each underlined word or phrase.

1. Did native people of America practice any <u>conservation</u> measures before other settlers came? . . . Native people were environmentally conscious because they lived close to the environment.
   a. communication with others
   b. protection of nature
   c. increase in size

2. Our people are taught to act and walk lightly upon this Earth in a <u>sacred</u> manner, making every step upon the Earth Mother as a prayer. . . .
   a. rough
   b. funny
   c. religious

3. Others don't realize how much care they took in the woods. In everything they did, they were <u>conscious</u> of the fact that if you disturb something, it will have <u>ramifications</u> through the whole web of life.

   a. aware   a. effects
   b. quiet   b. causes
   c. below   c. comparisons

4. But the Europeans came here with <u>conquest</u> in mind. They took what land they could take, bought what they could buy, and stole and fought for the rest.
   a. surrender
   b. control
   c. religion

5. The Earth and our fellow creatures are more valuable than all the <u>fancy</u> things we have.
   a. cheap and simple
   b. boring and unusual
   c. expensive and complicated

6. It should <u>horrify</u> all human beings that we are losing whole species of animals and birds.
   a. surprise
   b. shock
   c. amuse

7. When you're somebody's friend, you don't let anybody hurt him, you <u>stick up for</u> him.
   a. look for
   b. question
   c. defend

It takes eighteen pounds of coffee and twelve coffee trees to keep the average coffee drinker supplied for a year.

B Circle the letter of the correct answer.

1. If something you saw on TV <u>horrified</u> you, it was probably _____.
   a. shocking and unpleasant   **b.** funny and interesting

2. When would you be more likely to stay in a <u>fancy</u> hotel?
   a. on a camping trip   **b.** on your honeymoon

3. If a country acquired a piece of land by <u>conquest</u>, what was probably involved?
   a. a pleasant conversation   **b.** military force

4. If you make a mistake that has lots of <u>ramifications</u>, the mistake was _____ one.
   a. a serious   **b.** an unimportant

5. Which is a <u>sacred</u> place?
   a. a temple   **b.** a gym

6. When would you <u>stick up for</u> your friend?
   a. when someone is giving him or her a gift   **b.** when someone is accusing your friend of something he or she didn't do

7. If you care about the <u>conservation</u> of endangered animals, you _____.
   a. want to save endangered animals   **b.** don't care about endangered animals

8. If a <u>species</u> of bird lives only on one island, _____.
   a. all of that kind of bird live there   **b.** a few of that kind of bird live there

✓ Learning Homonyms

C Read these sentences. Write the meaning and part of speech of each underlined word. You may need to use your dictionary.

1. **a.** Please don't <u>step</u> on the carpet.
      Meaning: _____
      Part of speech: _____
   b. He ran up the <u>steps</u> two at a time.
      Meaning: _____
      Part of speech: _____

2. a. Please <u>point</u> to the correct answer.
Meaning: _____
Part of speech: _____

b. I don't understand the <u>point</u> of the story.
Meaning: _____
Part of speech: _____

3. a. This <u>land</u> belongs to my grandfather.
Meaning: _____
Part of speech: _____

b. The plane <u>landed</u> ten minutes ago.
Meaning: _____
Part of speech: _____

4. a. It isn't right to <u>subject</u> these people to your rules.
Meaning: _____
Part of speech: _____

b. The <u>subject</u> for this discussion is crime in our society.
Meaning: _____
Part of speech: _____

5. a. I'm tired. I need to take a <u>rest</u> now.
Meaning: _____
Part of speech: _____

b. She <u>rested</u> her head on his shoulder.
Meaning: _____
Part of speech: _____

Talk It Over

Discuss these questions as a class.

1. According to Manitonquat, native people everywhere feel that the Earth is spiritually alive and that we may live with the Earth, but we do not own it. Do you agree with this philosophy? Why or why not?
2. Chief Seattle also said, "You must remember that the land is sacred, and you must teach your children that it is sacred." Why is it important to teach our children about the land?
3. Here are the last three questions in the interview. How would you answer each one?
   a. What needs to be done for the Earth?
   b. What do we need to do to be friends with the Earth?
   c. What does it mean to be friends with the Earth?

Ninety percent of all trash can be recycled.

Read this excerpt from a speech given by a holy woman of the Wintu Indians of California. As you read, think about the similarities between her beliefs and those of Manitonquat. Then discuss the questions that follow in a small group.

> The white people never cared for land or deer or bear. When we Indians kill meat, we eat it all up. When we dig roots, we make little holes. When we burn grass for grasshoppers, we don't ruin things. We shake down for nuts like acorns and pine nuts. We don't chop down the trees. We only use dead wood. But the white people plow up the ground, pull down the trees, kill everything. The tree says, "Don't. I am sore. Don't hurt me." But they chop it down and cut it up. The spirit of the land hates them. They blast out trees and stir it up to their depths. They saw up the trees. That hurts them. The Indians never hurt anything, but the white people destroy all. They blast rocks and scatter them on the ground. The rock says, "Don't. You are hurting me." But the white people pay no attention. When Indians use rocks, they take little round ones for their cooking. . . . How can the spirit of the Earth like the white man? Everywhere the white man has touched it, it is sore.

1. Why does the holy woman criticize the way white people treat animals and land?
2. How would you describe Native Americans' relationship with the Earth? What about their attitude toward the environment?
3. In what ways is it similar to or different from your own attitude?

Our Endangered Wildlife

Before You Read

A Discuss these questions with a partner.

1. Do you know of any animals that are in danger of dying out, or becoming extinct? Give some examples.
2. Read the first paragraph of the article. What kinds of responsibility do you think humans have toward the Earth?

✓ **Previewing and Predicting**

B Preview the article by looking at the title and picture. Skim the first paragraph and the first sentence of the other paragraphs. Make some predictions about the content of the article. Write your ideas on the lines.

_____

_____

_____

C Learn the meanings of the following words and phrase before you read the article.

vanished (1)   accelerating (5)

tragic (3)   habitats (6)

wildlife (3)   chain reaction (8)

microscopic (3)

Our Endangered Wildlife

1   Before this day ends, approximately 45 different kinds of plants and animals will die out. A month from now, 1,400 more species will be gone. Within a year, the number of vanished species will total about 17,500. Scientists provide these estimates, which represent the most *hopeful* case. The actual numbers may prove to be much higher.

2   Among the vanishing species are African elephants. The reduction in the African elephant population has

been caused by two primary factors: the killing of elephants for ivory (poaching); and competition with humans for land. Ivory hunters continue to kill elephants for their ivory, even though it is illegal. Farmers in overcrowded countries squeeze elephant herds into spaces too small to support them. In 1930, there were between 5 million and 10 million African elephants. Twenty years ago, 1.5 million elephants roamed the African countryside. Now perhaps only 500,000 remain.

3   Loss of the elephants, nearly everyone agrees, would be tragic. Even worse, say scientists, would be the loss of smaller species of wildlife. Grass and other small plants contribute oxygen. Small animals such as worms and termites are nature's recyclers. They convert organic matter (dead plants, animal waste, etc.) into valuable nutrients for rich and fertile soil. The loss of microscopic species is unfortunate, too. "It's the tiny species that really run the planet," says Dr. Thomas Lovejoy, a biologist and conservationist. For example, certain microorganisms such as bacteria make digestion possible. Fungi give us penicillin and other medicines.

4   Huge numbers of unknown plants and animals are also in danger. The Earth, according to various estimates, supports between 5 million and 80 million species. Of these, scientists have found and named only about $1\frac{1}{2}$ million. "Species are disappearing before we have a chance to learn how they might benefit the rest of the planet," says Dr. Lovejoy. The disappearance of these plants and animals has unfortunate consequences. For one thing, we lose thousands of kinds of tropical plants that could help feed a growing world population. We also lose the medicinal benefits these species might hold. About 40 percent of prescription medicines come from ingredients found in plants. Some animals also provide the ingredients to make medicines.

5   Dr. Lovejoy says, "It's natural for species to become extinct over millions of years. What's unnatural is that humans are speeding up the process many times over." How are they doing this? People are accelerating the process of animal extinction in several ways.

6   First of all, people threaten the survival of animal species by destroying their habitats. As human populations grow, people build houses and factories in fields and woods, destroying wildlife and animal habitats. If the animals can't find a new place to live, they die out. For example, humans are cutting down bamboo forests.

Many rare animals depend on bamboo for food and shelter. In Asia, the giant panda eats only bamboo. In Africa, the mountain gorilla depends on bamboo for most of its diet. In parts of Africa, Asia, and South America, many endangered species of animals and birds rely on bamboo as part of their diet. As you can see, when a plant disappears, animals that depend on it for food or shelter also suffer. In turn, species that depend on those animals are affected. "All life is interconnected," cautions Dr. Lovejoy.

7   Overhunting is another way that humans are causing some animals to become extinct. In some areas of the world, the parts of rare animals are worth a lot of money. Some people will pay more than $1,000 for a single horn from a rhinoceros. This encourages hunters to kill rhinos even though the animals face extinction. Other animals that are threatened with extinction from overhunting include the blue whale, the mountain gorilla, and the cheetah.

8   Humans are also polluting the air, water, and soil. The effect of pollution on animal species is like a chain reaction. For example, when waste from factories is dumped into rivers, the rivers become polluted, causing the fish that live in the rivers to be poisoned and die. Birds that eat the poisoned fish become poisoned themselves. Once they are poisoned, these birds cannot lay strong, healthy eggs. Fewer and fewer new birds are born.

9   Is there time to prevent disaster? Just barely, say scientists. Worldwide action will be difficult and costly. But scientists agree that action must be taken—quickly. The clock is ticking. . . .   ■

After You Read

Comprehension Check

A Circle the letter of the correct answer.

1. The article mainly discusses _____.
   a. the importance of African elephants
   b. the causes and effects of disappearing wildlife
   c. the hunting of elephants and rhinos
2. The author thinks that _____.
   a. we should only be concerned with the threat to large animals
   b. there isn't time to prevent the destruction of wildlife
   c. the loss of smaller species is a very serious problem
3. Which causes a chain reaction?
   a. when waste from factories is dumped into rivers
   b. when African elephants roam the countryside
   c. when mountain gorillas eat bamboo
4. Which is a natural process?
   a. humans destroying animal habitats
   b. species becoming extinct over millions of years
   c. humans speeding up the process of extinction

5. What can happen when a plant disappears?
   a. The animals that depend on it suffer.
   b. Humans can make more medicines.
   c. The price of ivory increases.
6. Which animal does NOT depend on bamboo in some way?
   a. giant pandas
   b. blue whales
   c. mountain gorillas

SKILL FOR SUCCESS

Understanding Cause and Effect

When you read, it is often important to understand the **causes** and/or **effects** of an event. When you want to find the causes (reasons), ask yourself, "Why did the event happen?" When you are looking for the effects (results), ask yourself, "What happened because of the event?"

Study these words and phrases that signal cause-and-effect relationships:

as a result	consequently
because	due to
bring about	effect(s)
cause(s)	therefore
consequence(s)	thus

B In "Our Endangered Wildlife," the author discusses the ways that humans are causing the extinction of wildlife. He also mentions some of the effects of the loss of wildlife. Answer each question with information from the article.

1. What two reasons does the author give for the reduction in populations of African elephants?
   a. _____
   b. _____

2. What are two effects of the disappearance of unknown plants and animals?
   a. _____
   b. _____

3. What are three causes of animal extinction that humans are involved in?
   a. _____
   b. _____
   c. _____

Vocabulary Practice

A Match each word or phrase with the correct definition.

Word or Phrase	Definition
_____ 1. wildlife	a. a plant or animal's natural environment
_____ 2. chain reaction	b. a series of events, each of which causes the next one
_____ 3. vanish	c. to make something happen at a faster rate
_____ 4. microscopic	d. animals and plants that live in natural conditions
_____ 5. habitat	e. to disappear suddenly
_____ 6. tragic	f. extremely small
_____ 7. accelerate	g. sad, terrible

B Complete each sentence with the correct word or phrase from Exercise A.

1. African elephants are only one example of a species that is beginning to _____.

2. Bacteria, fungi, and other _____ organisms are extremely important to life on planet Earth.

3. Unless we do something soon, the extinction of species will continue to _____.

4. Unfortunately, many animals die out when humans destroy their _____.

5. The way we are hurting the environment is _____.

6. Pollution and overhunting are ways humans are threatening birds and other _____.

7. The effects of pollution on animals cause a _____, with one effect causing another problem.

Understanding Word Parts: The Prefix *micro-*

The prefix *micro-* is added to a word to mean "very small." For example, in this chapter you learned that the word *microscopic* means "extremely small."

C Write a definition for each word. Use your dictionary to help you.

1. microbiology _____

2. microchip _____

3. microorganism _____

4. microphone _____

5. microwave _____

6. microscope _____

D Complete each sentence with the correct word(s) from Exercise C.

1. The _____ for this computer is made in California.

2. This _____ is so small that you can only see it under a _____.

3. The singer is using a _____ so everyone in the audience can hear her.

4. I learned how bacteria make digestion possible in a _____ course.

5. I'll cook the popcorn in the _____ oven.

The birds of the world are disappearing. Two-thirds of all species of birds are on the decline, and thousands of species are threatened with extinction.

Write a Summary

Read the passage. Then write a one-paragraph summary of the passage. Use the questions that follow to help you.

Elephants in Danger

In 1989, the United Nations created a plan to help save elephants from becoming extinct. The plan made it illegal to trade ivory from elephant tusks. Before 1989, more than 70,000 elephants were killed every year for their tusks, and the elephant population decreased by 50 percent. But after the plan was created, no one could kill elephants or sell their tusks.

Now, however, elephants might be in danger once again. The governments of several African countries want to begin the legal ivory trade again to help their countries' economies. They want to sell ivory they already have. There would be strict controls to monitor where the ivory comes from, but environmental groups worry that the sale of ivory will increase demand for ivory around the world. This could mean more elephants will be killed.

The wildlife groups will have to work extra hard to make sure elephants don't become extinct. ∎

1. What did the United Nations do in 1989 to help elephants?
2. Why are elephants in danger again?
3. Why do some African governments want to begin trading ivory again?

_____

_____

_____

_____

Make a Poster

In a small group, choose an animal that is in danger of becoming extinct. Copy or draw a picture of the animal on a poster. Use the Internet or library to find some facts about the animal. List at least five facts about the animal on your poster. Include facts about the animal's habitat and diet. Share your poster with your classmates.

The Heat Is On!

Before You Read

A Discuss these questions with a partner.

  1. Do you believe that the world is getting warmer? Are you concerned about it? Why or why not?
  2. Do you think it is possible for humans to affect climate? If so, how?
  3. How might changes in climate affect your everyday life?

✓ **Reading with a Purpose**

B You are going to read an article about global warming. Write three questions you hope will be answered in the article.

  1. _____

  2. _____

  3. _____

C Review the list of cause-and-effect signal words on page 171. Look for these signals as you read the article. Underline the signal words as you read.

D Learn the meanings of the following words before you read the article.

convinced (1)   grave (4)
vital (2)   treaty (5)
intensifying (3)   pledge (5)
countless (4)

The Heat Is On!
Welcome to Life in the Greenhouse

by David Bjerklie

1   Most scientists who study climate think that our world is getting warmer.

The three warmest years on record have all occurred since 1998. Nine of the ten warmest years have occurred in the past decade. And nineteen of the warmest twenty since 1980. Of course, nature has brought about dramatic changes in the Earth's climate in the past, such as the Ice Ages[1]. But most scientists are convinced that humans are responsible for the current warming trend and are making it worse.

What Causes Global Warming?

2   Global warming is the gradual increase in the world's temperature. In order to understand the cause of global warming, it is important to understand a process that scientists call *the greenhouse effect*. It works like this. The Earth's atmosphere is the mixture of gases that surrounds the

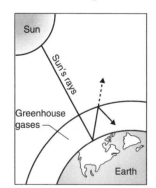

The greenhouse effect

planet. The atmosphere acts like the glass of a greenhouse. It lets sunlight in and keeps the right amount of heat from escaping. The greenhouse effect is vital because without it, the Earth would be too cold for plants and animals (including humans) to live.

3   But the greenhouse effect is a delicate process, and people are intensifying the natural greenhouse effect. When people burn fuels such as coal and oil to produce power for cities, factories, homes, and cars, enormous amounts of polluting gases enter the atmosphere. By pumping more and more polluting gases (often called greenhouse gases) into the atmosphere, humans are making the greenhouse effect too strong. In other words, we are causing the Earth to become warmer. And the effects on climate have clearly started, according to Kevin Trenberth of the National Center for Atmospheric Research. "We are already seeing fewer frost days, heavier rains, and more droughts and heat waves," Trenberth said.

The Effects of Global Warming

4   Scientists worry that the trend in global warming could get worse. If that happens, the effects could be disastrous. Higher temperatures could cause droughts in some places where important crops such as wheat and corn can be grown. The result would be that some people may not have

---

[1] **Ice Age** – a period of time when the temperature was very cold and large parts of the Earth were covered in ice

enough food to eat. Countless species of plants and animals could face big disturbances of their habitats and even extinction. Scientists also worry that global warming will cause mountaintop glaciers² and the ice sheets in the Arctic and Antarctic to melt. This will result in the rise of sea levels around the globe. The effects of rising sea levels would be grave. Water would cover coasts and low-lying islands; therefore, land where hundreds of millions of people live would be lost.

What Can We Do to Slow Global Warming?

5   Most scientists agree that the best way to slow global warming is to reduce the amount of greenhouse gases that are put into the atmosphere. That would mean businesses and governments need to come up with new technologies that limit the production of greenhouse gases. Many countries have already signed a treaty called the Kyoto Protocol, which requires them to pledge to reduce their greenhouse emissions³. One thing is certain: The entire world will have to work to turn down the heat. "Climate change is truly a global issue," says Trenberth, "and one that may prove to be humanity's greatest challenge." ■

² **glacier** – a large area of ice

³ **emissions** – gases that are sent out to the atmosphere

After You Read

Comprehension Check

A   Circle the letter of the correct answer.

1. The Earth's climate _____.
   a. has changed many times in the past
   b. stays constant, rarely changing at all
   c. probably won't change in the future
2. Which is NOT true about the greenhouse effect?
   a. It is necessary for life on our planet.
   b. It keeps heat and sunlight away from Earth.
   c. It could cause problems if it becomes stronger.
3. What could happen if global warming continues?
   a. Plants and animals will suffer.
   b. The Earth will become colder.
   c. Sea levels will fall.
4. What is the Kyoto Protocol?
   a. a treaty that requires countries to promise to reduce their greenhouse gas emissions
   b. a new type of technology that produces less greenhouse gas
   c. a place where important crops such as wheat, rice, and corn are grown

5. Kevin Trenberth _____.
   a. thinks there is too much emphasis on global warming
   b. believes global warming is a very serious issue
   c. hopes no more countries will participate in the Kyoto Protocol

SKILL FOR SUCCESS

Understanding Chain Reactions
Sometimes cause-and-effect relationships are complicated. The effect of one event can become the cause of another event. When a group of related events cause another event, it is called a **chain reaction**. Making a chart of the causes and effects will help you see the relationships more easily.

B Complete the chain reaction chart with items from the list.

- droughts in some places
- extinction of some animals
- melting of glaciers and Arctic ice cap
- huge amounts of polluting gases emitted
- some crops cannot be grown
- flooding of coastlines and islands where people live

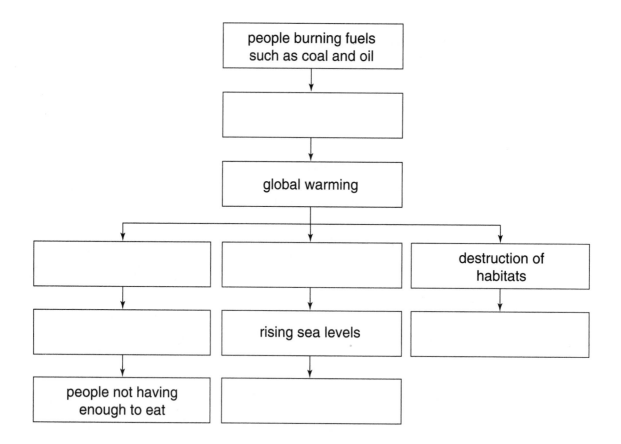

✓ **Summarizing**

C Write a one-paragraph summary of the article. Use these questions to help you.

1. What do most scientists think about the Earth's changing climate?
2. What is making the trend worse?
3. What will be affected by global warming?
4. How can we slow down global warming?

_____

_____

_____

_____

_____

Vocabulary Practice

A Complete each sentence with the correct word.

convinced	pledge
countless	treaty
grave	vital
intensify	

1. I'm worried about the economic stability of the country. Its situation is _____.

2. I'm _____ that we need to stop burning so much fuel.

3. I'm sick of this song. They've played it _____ times in the past week.

4. The two countries signed a peace _____.

5. It's _____ that you take this medicine every six hours.

6. Please _____ your support to help make this project a reality.

7. The greenhouse effect may be a natural process, but people _____ the situation.

✓ Learning Synonyms and Antonyms

B For each pair of words, circle *S* if they are synonyms or *A* if they are antonyms.

1. grave	serious	S	A
2. convinced	certain	S	A
3. intensify	weaken	S	A
4. countless	numerous	S	A
5. pledge	promise	S	A
6. vital	unimportant	S	A
7. treaty	disagreement	S	A

SKILL FOR SUCCESS ✓

Using *Therefore* and *Because*

Therefore means "for that reason." It is used to connect two sentences when the second sentence is the result of the first sentence. *Because* means "for the reason that." It is used to show cause.

C Match each effect with its cause.

Effect

_____ 1. Rivers become polluted.

_____ 2. Droughts occur in some places.

_____ 3. Polluting gases are produced.

_____ 4. They can't lay healthy eggs.

_____ 5. Sea levels rise.

Cause

a. The Earth's temperature increases.

b. Glaciers melt.

c. Humans burn fuels.

d. Factories dump waste into rivers.

e. Birds eat the poisoned fish.

D Combine the causes and effects in Exercise C to make new sentences. Use *because* or *therefore*. (Note: When the word *therefore* is used in the middle of a sentence, put a semicolon between the two sentences and a comma after the word *therefore*.)

1. *Rivers become polluted because factories dump waste into them.*

   OR

   Factories dump waste into rivers; therefore, they become polluted.

2. _____

3. _____

4. _____

5. _____

Make a World Earth Day Stamp

In a small group, create a World Earth Day stamp. Think of a theme for your stamp. For example, the stamp could honor a person, a place, or an idea. Decorate your stamp, including the country name and value of the stamp. Show your stamp to your classmates.

UNIT 7 Tie It All Together

Discussion

Discuss these questions in a small group.

1. What do you think is the biggest environmental problem that your country faces? What is being done to solve it?
2. Read and discuss the following quote of naturalist John Muir. Do you agree or disagree with it?
   "When one tugs at a single thing in nature, he finds it attached to the rest of the world."
3. When a Russian cosmonaut viewed the Earth from space, he wrote, "It does not matter what country you look at. We are all Earth's children, and we should treat her as our mother." How are his ideas similar to those of the Native Americans?

Just for Fun

The word ENVIRONMENTAL has thirteen letters. Use these letters to make as many other words as you can. You may not use the same letter twice in a word unless it appears twice in *environmental*. Do not use proper names or foreign words.

_____   _____

_____   _____

_____   _____

_____   _____

_____   _____

Video Activity   **The Eagles Return**

This video reports on the bald eagle and the effort to bring the species back from the edge of extinction. Think back to your reading in this unit. What threatens many animal species? Can you guess what has threatened the bald eagle?

A Study these words and phrases. Then watch the video.

come to fruition	offspring	soaring
interference	paying off	suburbs
national emblem	pesticides	

B Read these questions and then watch the video again. Circle the correct answers. (Some questions have more than one answer.)

1. Why did the attitude about protecting the bald eagle change?
   a. It's a national emblem.
   b. It was almost extinct.
   c. It's a courageous bird.
2. What has threatened the bald eagle?
   a. pesticides
   b. cutting down trees
   c. hunting
3. What has happened to the bald eagle population in California?
   a. It has stayed the same.
   b. It has gone up.
   c. It has gone down.
4. How many bald eagle nests were there in New York at the time of the report?
   a. very few
   b. a single nest
   c. 80

C Discuss these questions with a partner or in a small group.

1. What kind of person can help an endangered species recover as Peter Nye helped the eagles in New York State?
2. If you had the chance to help an endangered species, which one would you choose? Why?

Reader's Journal

Think about the topics and ideas you have read about and discussed in this unit. Pick a topic from the list, one of the discussion questions in the unit, or an idea of your own. Write about it for ten to twenty minutes.

- threats our planet faces
- ways people, organizations, and countries are trying to solve the problems facing our planet
- effects of global warming

Complete each sentence with the correct word or phrase.

A   conquests   countless   species   tragic
convince   habitats   stick up for   treaty

1. Military _____ have often changed the course of history.

2. Humans have destroyed the natural _____ of many
_____ .

3. We signed a peace _____ after the war.

4. Felipe spent _____ hours renovating his house.

5. It was just a _____ accident.

6. The job of a defense lawyer is to _____ the jury that his
or her client is innocent.

7. It's important to _____ your friends when they are being
attacked.

B   accelerated   conscious   fancy   vital
chain reaction   conservation   grave

1. Serena was _____ of the fact that she had to sell more
books.

2. Amy is working on a national _____ project to protect
the beaches and forests.

3. The effect of pollution on plants and animal species causes a
_____ of destructive events.

4. Dr. Morales looked very _____ when he told me about
Stephania's problem.

5. Melanie _____ as she drove onto the freeway.

6. The new hotel they are building downtown will be very
_____ .

7. Nowadays, computers are considered _____ in the
airline industry.

C horrifying   microscopic   ramifications   vanished
    intensify   pledge   sacred   wildlife

1. After the hurricane, several countries made a(n) _____
to help with disaster relief.

2. The church choir will sing _____ music at our wedding.

3. The damage that the tornado caused was _____ .

4. There is a lot of _____ in the area around the Rocky
Mountains.

5. Bacteria are _____ . We can't see them with the naked
eye.

6. The police say the suspect _____ . They're looking for
him all throughout the city.

7. The economic _____ of rising oil prices are serious.

8. Spices _____ the flavor of many foods.

LIVING A LONG LIFE

The question of how to live to an old age has always fascinated people. Is there a secret to living a long life? What can we learn from older people? In this unit, you will read about some of the interesting new research into growing older, or aging, and some of the important things we can learn from older people.

Points to Ponder

Think about these questions and discuss them in a small group.

1. What do you think young people learn from older people?

2. What are some challenges that people face as they grow older?

3. What are the attitudes toward older people in your culture? Are older people respected? Ignored?

UNIT 8

CHAPTER 1

Discovering the Secrets to a Long Life

Before You Read

A Discuss these questions with a partner.

1. Do you know anyone who has lived more than 100 years? Have you ever discussed the secret to his or her long life?
2. An expedition is an organized journey that you take for a specific purpose. Have you ever been on an expedition to another country or another part of your country? If you have, where did you go? What did you learn? If you haven't, would you like to go on an expedition? Where would you like to go?

✓ **Using Background Knowledge**

B What do you think are the most important factors for living a long and healthy life? Write your ideas in the chart. Then discuss your ideas with a partner. Write his or her ideas in the chart. Did you include any of the same factors?

	Your Factors	**Your Partner's Factors**
1.		
2.		
3.		
4.		
5.		

C Learn the meanings of the following words and phrases before you read the article.

hung out with (1)   turns it on its head (4)

toddlers (1)   foremost (6)

rich (3)   pioneer (7)

quest (3)   extraordinarily (7)

DISCOVERING THE SECRETS TO A LONG LIFE

Martha Pickerill

1 Ushi Okushima has hung out with the same group of friends almost every day of her life since they were toddlers. Now Ushi and her friends are 103 years old. Not only does Ushi have great friends, she also has a new job, and she has just started wearing perfume because she has a new boyfriend!

2 Ushi Okushima lives in Okinawa, Japan, where people live seven years longer than the average American. Okinawans live longer than anyone else in Japan, too. According to the Japanese government, 457 Okinawans are at least 100 years old. That means for every 100,000 people who live on the island, there are 34.7 centenarians. That's the highest ratio[1] in the world.

3 Explorer and adventurer Dan Buettner wanted to learn how Okinawans lived such long lives. "We want these people to teach us what makes a difference in the quality and length of their life," Buettner said. "Do they dance? Play chess? Play a musical instrument? Meditate[2] or pray?" But he didn't just sit in his office doing research. Instead, he led an expedition to Okinawa to figure out Okinawans' recipe for living such long, rich, healthful lives. However, his wasn't an ordinary expedition. On a typical expedition, a group of people travel to a part of the world for exploration or scientific research. They have adventures and then return to share their stories. In traditional expeditions, only the people who actually go on the expedition can participate. But on Buettner's expedition, anyone who is interested in the quest can be part of the story by participating in it. How did he do it?

---

[1] **ratio** – the relationship between two different numbers or amounts

[2] **meditate** – to make yourself feel calm by being silent and still and thinking only about one thing such as a sound

An Interactive Expedition

4   To get everyone involved in the expedition, Buettner created an interactive Website called Blue Zones. (*Blue Zones* is Buettner's term for the places where people live the longest, healthiest lives.) By clicking on the Website, you can take part in the expedition without leaving your home. The message that greets you on the Website is "Welcome to a Brave New World of Exploration. The Blue Zones Expedition takes the old way of exploration and turns it on its head."

5   For three weeks in October 2005, people at home and in schools used their computers to direct the live expedition team in Okinawa, Japan. They voted on the place in Okinawa that the Blue Zones team should explore next. The following day, the team put information on the Website and gave a written report and a video about the people they met on their most recent adventure. The goal was to review the clues from each day's discoveries to see what kind of choices and activities helped the Okinawans live so well, and so long.

6   The fourteen-member team in Okinawa included medical experts, filmmakers, photographers, journalists, and technology experts to help dig up the facts and deliver them on the Website each day. All the members of the team prepared for the expedition by researching Okinawa and meeting some of the people who live there. The team included some of the world's top experts in the fields of medicine and gerontology (the scientific study of aging). Dr. Greg Plotnikoff, the world's foremost expert in Japanese alternative medicine[3] led the medical team. Dr. Craig Willcox, who has been studying Okinawan centenarians for more than a decade, was a consultant for the team. His book *The Okinawa Program* is a *New York Times* Best Seller. The book documents the diet, exercise, and lifestyle practices of the Okinawans. The team also included creative filmmakers and journalists Damian Petrou, Tom Adair, and Eric Luoma.

7   Dan Buettner is a pioneer in both exploration and education. He is also an athlete, holding three world records for long-distance bicycle journeys. He has completed more than twelve online quests since 1995, from South America to Africa to China. In the next few years, Buettner will explore three more places where the people live extraordinarily long lives.

8   "At the end," said Buettner, "we want to see how these quests bring together the imagination and the idea-generating power of a big online audience to find something that no one knew before." That sounds like a goal that could make life very exciting for Buettner and his fellow explorers.

---

[3] **alternative medicine** – medical treatments that are different from usual medical practices, including vitamins, spiritual healing, herbal teas, and acupuncture

After You Read

Comprehension Check

A Read these statements. If a statement is true according to the article, write *T* on the line. If it is false, write *F*.

_____ 1. Ushi Okushima has had the same group of friends her whole life.

_____ 2. According to the Japanese government, Okinawa has the lowest ratio of old people in the world.

_____ 3. Dan Buettner wanted to learn how so many Okinawans live such long lives.

_____ 4. Buettner created an interactive Website so people could participate in his quest.

_____ 5. Dr. Greg Plotnikoff knows a lot about Japanese alternative medicine.

_____ 6. A Blue Zones expedition to Okinawa will take place next October.

_____ 7. Buettner has led quests to South America, Africa, and China.

✓ Making Inferences

B Check (✔) the statements that are inferences you can make based on the information in the article.

❏ 1. Dan Buettner is curious about how people live long and healthy lives.

❏ 2. Diet and exercise are important factors in leading a long and healthy life.

❏ 3. Many people bought the book *The Okinawa Program*.

❏ 4. Okinawa is not the only place where the people live extraordinarily long lives.

❏ 5. Dan Buettner can ride very long distances on a bicycle.

❏ 6. People participating in the quest learned about Okinawa by reading reports and watching videos on the Internet.

❏ 7. Damian Petrou led the photography team.

❏ 8. It is important to do research before going on an expedition.

9. There are many expeditions like the Blue Zones expedition to Okinawa.

10. Blue Zones expeditions are a new way of exploration.

11. All Okinawans live to be 100.

Vocabulary Practice

A Circle the letter of the word or phrase that is closest in meaning to the underlined word or phrase in each sentence.

1. Ushi Okushima has <u>hung out with</u> the same group of friends almost every day since they were <u>toddlers</u>.

   a. spent time with   a. old friends
   b. spent money on   b. college students
   c. worked for   c. young children

2. But on Buettner's expedition, anyone who is interested in the <u>quest</u> can be part of the story by participating in it.

   a. Internet
   b. search
   c. old age

3. He led an expedition to Okinawa to figure out Okinawans' recipe for living such long, <u>rich</u>, healthful lives.

   a. wealthy
   b. full
   c. poor

4. The Blue Zones Expedition takes the old way of exploration and <u>turns it on its head</u>.

   a. makes it the opposite of what it was
   b. keeps it the same as it was
   c. looks the other way

5. Dr. Greg Plotnikoff, the world's <u>foremost</u> expert in Japanese alternative medicine, led the medical team.

   a. most important
   b. least known
   c. youngest

6. Dan Buettner is a <u>pioneer</u> in both exploration and education.

   a. an uninterested leader
   b. a recent graduate
   c. one of the first people to do something

7. In the next few years, Buettner will explore three more places where the people live <u>extraordinarily</u> long lives.
   a. slightly
   b. usually
   c. extremely

SKILL FOR SUCCESS

Understanding Word Parts: Root Words; the Suffix *-ology*
Many English words have **roots** in Latin and Greek. Although words change over time, you can still see certain roots in English. Learning the meaning of common roots will help you figure out the definitions of unfamiliar words.

When you add the suffix *-ology* to a root, it means "the study of something." In this chapter, you learned that *gerontology* means "the study of aging." The root *geront-* means "old age." When you add the suffix *-ology*, you get the word *gerontology*.

Remember: When you add the suffix *-ist* to a word, it means "someone who studies something."

B Complete the chart. Add *-ology* to each root word to form the name of the field of study. Then add *-ist* to form the word for a person who works in that field. Follow the example. You may need to use your dictionary to help with spelling.

Root word	Field of study	Job
1. anthr(o)- (man)	*anthropology*	*anthropologist*
2. cardi(o)- (heart)		
3. dermat(o)- (skin)		
4. neur(o)- (nerve)		
5. ge(o)- (earth)		
6. clima(t)- (climate)		

C Choose four words from the chart in Exercise B. Write a sentence for each word.

1. _____
2. _____
3. _____
4. _____

Make a Poster

Make and illustrate a poster about how to live a long life. Include at least three of your factors from Activity B on page 188. Think of a title for your poster and write it on the top. Share your poster with your classmates.

What Makes a Champion?

Most of us can point to someone in our lives who has served as a role model and source of strength and inspiration. Joe Lewis is a champion in martial arts. In "What Makes a Champion?" he talks about his father and the important lessons he learned from him.

Before You Read

A Discuss these questions with a partner.

1. Look at the title of the article. What do you think makes a champion? What are the most important qualities of a winner?
2. At the beginning of the article, Joe Lewis asks, "What does it mean to grow old? What does it mean to age?" How would you answer these questions?

B Learn the meanings of the following words and phrases before you read the article.

principle (3)   common sense (8)
endurance (3)   plain (8)
confidence (7)   regardless (9)
give up (7)

What Makes a Champion?

by Joe Lewis

1   What does it mean to grow old? What does it mean to age? Let me tell you about my father, John Gary Lewis. I  remember him about the age of fifty. Even then, he could work harder than men half his age. The fact that he never smoked or went to movies or parties made it easier for him, true. But he believed in working, even if he was sick or injured.

2   The fact is, he almost never got sick, and he never seemed to get hurt. He didn't believe in doctors. He was old-fashioned in every way. He believed in home care when you were sick. He did his farming without tractors because he thought they would damage the roots of the plants. He was a college professor in North Carolina for thirty years, full time, and when he wasn't teaching, he was out at his farm, working, sunup to sundown, never taking a vacation, day in and day out, year after year.

3   So my four brothers and I grew up in Raleigh in a tough family. We were guided by the principle that physical strength and endurance are key to survival. I still think of my father at fifty on his feet in the hot burning sun, outworking my brothers and me.

4   A long time afterward, when I turned fifty, I got into the ring and sparred[1] with some young kids, and I found it quite easy to beat them.

5   I have a sixty-two-year-old friend, Gene LaBell, a national judo champion, who can practice judo nonstop for a full hour. I've seen folks seventy and older who can still lift heavy weights. And I know members of the Santa Monica track club—guys forty-eight, forty-nine, and fifty years old—who can still run the 100 meters in ten seconds.

6   The trouble with most of us is that we're conditioned to start surrendering inside once we get between fifty and sixty. Our values and interests start to change, and it no longer matters so much who's the best, especially since we know it's unlikely to be us.

7   But why throw away your skills and talents just because you're a little older? There's something in each of us—call it spirit, energy, confidence, courage, heart, guts, backbone, intensity, or just a refusal to give up, like my old man. If you let this part of you begin to go to sleep, it will start working to take the rest of you to your grave.

8   We have to learn to live with fear, whether it's fear of death, fear of injury, fear of failure, or fear of being laughed at because we're competing with folks half our age. Common sense and a little reflection make it plain that none of this means a thing.

---

[1] **spar** – to practice boxing or martial arts with someone

9　When you are old, you can still be a winner, because winning truly means being the best of what you are, doing the best you can do, regardless of what anybody else says.

10　You don't give up. Like my father, who died at sixty-eight and never gave up, and who has been my life's example. He is no longer by me, but he is always with me.

11　Never give up. Never.　■

After You Read

Comprehension Check

A Circle the letter of the correct answer.

1. Which describes the way Joe Lewis feels about his father?
   a. He respects his father because he never gave up.
   b. He doesn't like the way his father lived his life.
   c. He can't understand why his father worked so hard.

2. What was Lewis's father like at the age of fifty?
   a. He only worked when he was sick and injured.
   b. He worked hard and never took a vacation.
   c. He was sick a lot of the time.

3. What was the guiding principle of Joe's life?
   a. Physical strength and endurance are key to survival.
   b. Physical strength is not as important as intelligence.
   c. Always believe in doctors.

4. According to Joe, what is the trouble with most of us beginning at about the age of fifty?
   a. We lose our value.
   b. We begin to give up on life.
   c. We go to sleep too early.

5. What personal quality does Joe say we must keep alive, especially as we age?
   a. spirit
   b. fear
   c. common sense

6. According to Joe Lewis, what does it take to be a winner?
   a. learning to live with fear
   b. living to age sixty-eight
   c. being the best you can be

✔ **Identifying Facts and Opinions**

B Decide if each statement is a fact or an opinion. Check (✔) the correct box.

	Fact	Opinion
1. Joe Lewis's father rarely got sick.		
2. We have to learn to live with fear.		
3. When you are old, you can still be a winner.		
4. The trouble with most of us is that we're conditioned to start surrendering inside once we get between fifty and sixty.		
5. Gene LaBell is a national judo champion.		
6. Some people in their forties can still run the 100 meters in ten seconds.		
7. Joe Lewis's father died at sixty-eight.		
8. Tractors always damage the roots of plants.		
9. Joe Lewis's father didn't smoke.		

Vocabulary Practice

A Match each word or phrase with the correct definition.

Word or Phrase

_____ 1. principle

_____ 2. endurance

_____ 3. confidence

_____ 4. plain

_____ 5. common sense

_____ 6. regardless

_____ 7. give up

Definition

a. the belief in your own or someone else's ability

b. to stop doing something

c. the ability to remain strong and patient even though you feel pain or have problems

d. in spite of

e. a rule or an idea that makes you behave in a particular way

f. clear and obvious

g. the ability to behave sensibly and make practical decisions

B Circle the letter of the correct answer.

1. If you <u>give up</u> smoking cigarettes, you _____ smoking.
   a. start   **b.** stop

2. If your friend has <u>common sense</u>, you would _____.
   a. ask him or her for advice **b.** never speak to him or her again

3. If you have the <u>confidence</u> that you will do well on an exam, you
   _____.
   a. believe you will pass   **b.** are afraid you will fail

4. If you quit your job <u>regardless</u> of the high pay, you quit _____ the
   pay.
   a. because of   **b.** in spite of

5. If you are guided by the <u>principle</u> that honesty is the best policy, you
   _____.
   a. usually tell the truth   **b.** approve of lying

6. If it is <u>plain</u> that your best friend is ignoring you, he or she is probably
   _____.
   a. calling you on the phone every day   **b.** not talking to you

7. To improve their physical <u>endurance</u>, some people _____
   a. run five miles a day   **b.** chew lots of gum

SKILL FOR SUCCESS

Learning Idioms: Parts of the Body
Words for **parts of the body** are often used figuratively. Joe Lewis uses the word *backbone* to mean "bravery and strength of character" and the word *guts* to mean "the ability to control fear and to deal with danger." English uses the words for body parts in many idioms.

C Match each idiom with the correct definition.

Idiom	Definition
_____ 1. break a leg	a. to memorize
_____ 2. see eye to eye	b. to promise not to tell a secret
_____ 3. keep your lips sealed	c. to have good luck
_____ 4. learn by heart	d. to agree on something
_____ 5. have cold feet	e. to be brave
_____ 6. keep your chin up	f. to be nervous about doing something

D Complete the conversations, using each idiom from Exercise C once.

1. **A:** I'm going to see your show tonight.
   B: I'm really nervous. I just can't _____ all the words to the songs.
   A: Well, _____. I know you'll be great. I won't say good luck. I'll just say, "_____."

2. **A:** My fiancé and I are always arguing. We don't seem to _____ on anything.
   B: Are you going to break up with him? It sounds like you _____ about the wedding.
   A: I do. I'll tell you a secret if you promise to _____.
   B: Of course. Just tell me.
   A: I'm going to give him the ring back tonight. I'm calling off the engagement.

Talk It Over

Discuss these questions as a class.

1. Joe Lewis says that his father has been his life's example. Do you have someone that you consider your life's example? If so, why is he or she an important role model for you?
2. Joe Lewis grew up in a family that was guided by the principle that physical strength and endurance are key to survival. Do you agree with this principle? Does your family have a guiding principle? What is it?
3. According to Joe Lewis, "The trouble with most of us is that we're conditioned to start surrendering inside once we get between fifty and sixty." Do you agree? Why or why not?
4. The article ends with the sentence, "He is no longer by me, but he is always with me." What do you think this means? Does this thought have significance for you?

Good News for the Aging Brain

Before You Read

A Discuss these questions with a partner.

1. What role do older people play in your life?
2. Do you know any older people who are still very active? How old are they? What do they do to keep active?
3. How do you think people can take better care of themselves to live longer lives?

✓ **Using Background Knowledge**

B You are going to read about the aging brain. Check (✓) the statements about this topic that you think are true. Then compare answers with a partner.

  ☐ 1. Scientists continue to learn new things about the aging brain.
  ☐ 2. Some elderly people accomplish amazing things.
  ☐ 3. Certain foods help your brain stay active longer.
  ☐ 4. It is not possible to learn new things later in life.
  ☐ 5. It is important for older people to get eight hours of sleep a night.
  ☐ 6. Doing puzzles and playing games are good for your brain.
  ☐ 7. Physical exercise is not very important for older people.

C Learn the meanings of the following words and phrase before you read the article.

competent (1)   come up with (4)
peaked (1)   fatigue (6)
feats (2)   concentrate (6)

Good News for the Aging Brain

1 Scientists have long believed that as people get older their brains become less and less able to perform certain tasks, remember information, and learn new ideas. However, new research on the brain may prove some of these ideas wrong. Today, scientists are discovering that in some ways the brain actually grows more competent with time. Jeffrey Kluger, a writer for *Time* magazine, reported that "Scientists used to think intellectual power peaked at age forty." But more recent studies show that the brain continues to develop during midlife (about ages thirty-five to sixty-five) and that older brains may even have some key advantages. One of the most surprising conclusions is that the human brain has the ability for learning throughout life.

2 There are lots of elderly people who are doing amazing things. All over the world, older people are breaking records and staying active both physically and mentally.

For example, the poet Stanley Kunitz won the National Book Award in 1995, when he was ninety years old. In 2000, he served as the poet laureate[1] of the United States. Today, at the age of 100, Kunitz still writes new poems. He is an inspiration to elderly people and proves that the aging brain is capable of great feats.

3 Ed Whitlock is another example of an elderly person doing things scientists never thought possible. At the age of seventy-four, Whitlock is one of the fastest marathon runners in the world and the fastest in his age group. Whitlock's performances in Canada and the United States have inspired elderly people all over the world to run greater distances. Whitlock says that it is not only his physical ability but also his mental attitude that allows him to continue to run so fast and for so long at an age that no one ever expected possible.

4 How do these people stay physically and mentally active and strong for so long? Scientists say that everything from what you eat to how much you study and exercise has an effect on the way your brain ages. Having a positive mental attitude is helpful, too. Of course, not every elderly person is writing poetry or running marathons. Scientists need to do more research to really understand how the brain develops over

[1] **poet laureate** – poet appointed every year to help people throughout the country appreciate poetry

time and why some people stay mentally active longer than others. But one thing seems true. The saying "Use it or lose it" applies to the aging human brain. And scientists have come up with a few things that older people can do to help their brains stay active for as long as possible.

5   For one thing, studies show that diet can affect mental activity throughout a person's life. For example, eating fish that live in cold water, such as salmon, may be good for the aging brain. Brightly colored fruits and vegetables, such as blueberries and broccoli, are also good. They contain antioxidants, chemicals that fight disease and aging in the body—including the brain.

6   Food is important, but so is sleep. Doctors recommend sleeping for at least eight hours every night to keep your brain working better. Like younger people, older people do not think as well when they are tired. Fatigue can have a bad effect on your memory and your ability to concentrate.

7   Studies also show that people who continue to read, write, and learn new things throughout their lives have a better chance of staying mentally active for longer. K. Warner Schaie studies the psychology of aging. He believes there are ways for older people to stay sharp. He suggests doing puzzles and playing games such as chess and bridge. Flexibility counts, too. People who stay mentally active are often those who do not insist that they "do things today as they did before," Schaie says.

8   Physical exercise is very important, too. Physical exercise seems to help mental functioning. This may be due to the improved circulation of your blood when you exercise. So if you want to keep your mind active for as long as possible, remember to eat well, exercise often, and never stop learning!

After You Read

Comprehension Check

A   Read these statements. If a statement is true according to the article, write *T* on the line. If it is false, write *F*.

_____ 1. Scientists are learning many new things about the human brain.

_____ 2. Diet has little effect on mental activity.

_____ 3. Scientists believe there are things you can do to stay mentally active longer.

_____ 4. Most elderly people write poetry and run marathons.

_____ 5. Exercise improves the circulation of your blood.

_____ 6. If you are older than sixty, doing crossword puzzles is a waste of time.

_____ 7. Stanley Kunitz and Ed Whitlock have both accomplished amazing feats in old age.

_____ 8. The antioxidants in brightly colored fruits cause disease.

✓ Making Inferences

B Check (✔) the statements you can infer to be true based on the information in the article. Discuss your answers with a partner.

❏ 1. Eating the cold-water fish mackerel may be beneficial to the aging brain.

❏ 2. Scientific conclusions never change.

❏ 3. Diet is more important than exercise for the aging brain.

❏ 4. Antioxidants are good for you.

❏ 5. Chess is better than bridge for your memory.

❏ 6. Both younger people and older people think better when they are well rested.

❏ 7. There are still things to learn about the aging brain.

Vocabulary Practice

A Circle the letter of the correct definition or synonym for each underlined word or phrase.

1. Today, scientists are discovering that in some ways the brain actually grows more <u>competent</u> with time.
   a. confused
   b. skilled
   c. useless

2. Scientists used to think intellectual power <u>peaked</u> at age forty.
   a. reached the highest level of skill
   b. dropped to the lowest level of skill
   c. stayed the same

3. He is an inspiration to elderly people and proves that the aging brain is capable of great <u>feats</u>.
   a. failures
   b. questions
   c. accomplishments

4. And scientists have <u>come up with</u> a few things that older people can do to help their brains stay active for as long as possible.
   a. discovered
   b. counted
   c. feared

5. Like younger people, older people do not think as well when they are tired. <u>Fatigue</u> can have a bad effect on your memory and your ability to concentrate.
   a. anger
   b. tiredness
   c. hunger

Learning Three-Word Verbs

You have learned that English has many two-word verbs such as *put on* and *get in*. When these words are used together, they mean something different from what they mean when they are used separately. English also has some **three-word verbs** that include a verb and two particles (prepositions or adverbs). For example, in this chapter, you learned that *come up with* means "to think of an idea."

B Study these common three-word verbs. Then complete each sentence with the correct verb. Be sure to use the correct form.

come down with—to become sick with an illness
get around to—to do something that you have intended to do for a long time
look down on—to regard as inferior
look up to—to respect and admire someone
look forward to—to feel pleased and excited about something that is going to happen
put up with—to tolerate something unpleasant

1. I am really _____ my vacation.
2. She is sneezing and coughing. I think she's _____ a cold.
3. Kathy has always _____ her older sister Megan. Megan is Kathy's role model.
4. I finally _____ cleaning the attic. I couldn't _____ the mess any longer.
5. You shouldn't _____ on people just because they are poor.

Read a Graph

Complete the paragraph with information from the graph.

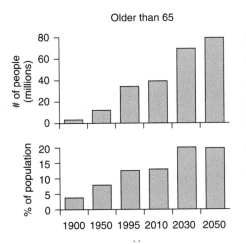

Older than 65

# of people (millions): 0, 20, 40, 60, 80

% of population: 0, 5, 10, 15, 20

1900 1950 1995 2010 2030 2050

Over the last 100 years, there has been a dramatic increase in the population of elderly (ages sixty-five and older) people. As shown in the graph, elderly people in the United States made up only 4.1 percent of the population in _____, but 8.1 percent in _____ and 12.8
  1.   2.
percent in 1995. By 2050, it is estimated that _____
                                                3.
percent of the population will be _____ years old or
                                   4.
older. This increase in the elderly population and the high incidence of age-related neurological disorders make it important to understand how the human brain ages.

Tie It All Together

Discussion

Discuss these questions in a small group.

1. Do you think older people have a responsibility to keep the values and traditions of their culture alive? If so, how can they do this?
2. Discuss these quotes. What do you think each one means?
   a. Philosopher Bernard Baruch said, "To me, old age is always fifteen years older than I am."
   b. Author and feminist Betty Freidan said, "Aging is not 'lost youth' but a new stage of opportunity and strength."
   c. Architect Frank Lloyd Wright said, "The longer I live, the more beautiful life becomes."

Just for Fun

Work as a class to figure out a solution to the following situation.

Your class has worked so hard learning English and progressed so well that someone is giving you one million dollars! He doesn't care how you divide the money or what you do with it. But he doesn't want you to know who he is, and he has three requests.

1. You must agree as a class on what to do with the money.
2. The money must all be used by the time you are sixty-five years old.
3. Each of you must e-mail him about your plans for the money.

As a class, decide how you are going to use the money. Then complete the e-mail.

Delete	Reply	Reply All	Forward	New	Mailboxes	Get Mail	Junk

To: Secretdonor@Englishprize.com
From:
 Subj:

_____

Dear Secret Donor,

Longevity Gene?

This video looks at why some people live longer than others. Scientists are continually making discoveries that give us information about aging. What kind of discovery do you think you will hear about in this video?

A Study these words and phrases. Then watch the video.

dealt   play the hand
gene   practices law
genetic   volunteer
longevity

B Read these statements and then watch the video again. Circle the sentence that best describes the main idea.

  a. The secret to living a long life is a combination of genes and lifestyle choices.
  b. Scientists have discovered a gene called E-4 that may help fight certain illnesses.
  c. Centenarians know that keeping active will prolong their lives.

C Discuss these questions with a partner or in a small group.

  1. If you could sit down and talk with a centenarian, what would you ask him or her?
  2. Do people in your family live very long lives? Do you expect to live to a very old age? What are some advantages to living a long life? What are some disadvantages?
  3. How much do you think attitude or expectation about longevity affects the length of a lifetime?

Reader's Journal

Think about the topics and ideas you have read about and discussed in this unit. Pick a topic from the list, one of the discussion questions in the unit, or an idea of your own. Write about it for ten to twenty minutes.

- things you can learn from older people
- an older person you respect
- ways to stay healthy in old age

Vocabulary Self-Test

Complete each sentence with the correct word or phrase.

A come up with   endurance   regardless   toddlers
confidence   fatigue   rich

1. After their night on the mountain, they were cold and weak from
   _____, but they were not injured.

2. It is possible for older people to lead _____ and fulfilling
   lives.

3. Chris and Jann have been friends since they were _____.

4. My boss said he will not change his mind _____ of what
   anyone else says.

5. My husband has no _____ in my driving.

6. I couldn't _____ a good excuse for being so late to class.

7. Jogging could help increase your _____.

B concentrate   hang out with   plain   quest
gave up   pioneers   principle

1. My grandfather's ancestors were _____ in the settling of
   the western United States.

2. Throughout history, many people have gone on a _____
   to find the secret to staying young.

3. It's quite _____ that you don't agree with me.

4. Vladimir told me that long ago he _____ trying to teach
   Jane to speak Russian.

5. I've been very busy lately and haven't had time to _____
   my friends.

6. She lives by the _____ that honesty and hard work are key to success.

7. Please turn the TV down. I'm trying to study, and I can't _____ with all the noise.

C common sense   extraordinarily   foremost   turned it on its head
competent   feat   peak

1. I ran the marathon! It was a great _____ for me.

2. For someone who is so _____ at work, Olive has very little _____.

3. Charlotte is the _____ authority on language-acquisition theory.

4. Joe took the system we have been using at work for ten years and _____.

5. I just heard a(n) _____ funny story about a man who walked all the way around the world.

6. According to new research, some of our mental abilities don't _____ until age forty.

Vocabulary Self-Tests Answer Key

Unit 1
(pages 23–24)

A 1. associated with
2. attractive
3. ethnic
4. signify
5. made up
6. system
7. complicated

B 1. cuisine
2. generations
3. vary
4. ill
5. deal
6. documents
7. unreliable

C 1. instead of
2. authority
3. rude
4. flavorings
5. pass down
6. appreciation
7. extensive
8. represent

Unit 2
(pages 51–52)

A 1. intrigued
2. speculate
3. estimated
4. biologist
5. sensation

B 1. figure out
2. Agriculture
3. weapon
4. on purpose
5. silent
6. fascinate

C 1. carve
2. theory
3. belongings
4. disaster
5. tiny
6. shocked

D 1. cooperated
2. evidence
3. sparked
4. descendant
5. magnificent
6. baffled

Unit 3
(pages 75–76)

A 1. lively
2. client
3. inspirational
4. solo
5. kick off
6. renovate
7. accomplished
8. celebrity

B 1. patient
2. composers
3. praised
4. charities
5. genius
6. essential
7. overcome

C 1. cause
2. victims
3. annoying
4. humanitarian
5. delighted
6. masterpiece
7. calming
8. committed

Unit 4
(pages 103–104)

A 1. tricky
2. vehicle
3. invested/make a mint
4. fragrance
5. mood
6. fuel

B 1. run out of
2. enticed
3. alternative
4. Word of mouth
5. practical
6. tips
7. volunteer
8. selling like hotcakes

C 1. proof
2. fake
3. catching on
4. convert
5. stinks
6. led by the nose
7. flexible

Unit 5
(pages 131–132)

A 1. Animated
2. brought a halt to
3. character
4. linked
5. big hit
6. remodel

B 1. heroine
2. transmitted
3. pilot/theme
4. craze
5. swap

6. categories
7. documentary

C 1. spin-off
   2. Prime-time
   3. episode
   4. trial and error
   5. eliminated
   6. critique
   7. interfere
   8. diversity

Unit 6
(pages 156–157)

A 1. misfortune
   2. stick to
   3. security
   4. acquired
   5. legend
   6. hoax
   7. hung up on

B 1. illusion
   2. weird/quirks
   3. pass up
   4. eager
   5. feast
   6. rituals

C 1. notion/skipping
   2. reputation
   3. rearranged
   4. banned
   5. blamed
   6. tragedy

Unit 7
(pages 184–185)

A 1. conquests
   2. habitats/species
   3. treaty
   4. countless
   5. tragic
   6. convince
   7. stick up for

B 1. conscious
   2. conservation
   3. chain reaction
   4. grave
   5. accelerated
   6. fancy
   7. vital

C 1. pledge
   2. sacred
   3. horrifying
   4. wildlife

5. microscopic
6. vanished
7. ramifications
8. intensity

Unit 8
(pages 208–209)

A 1. fatigue
   2. rich
   3. toddlers
   4. regardless
   5. confidence
   6. come up with
   7. endurance

B 1. pioneers
   2. quest
   3. plain
   4. gave up
   5. hang out with
   6. principle
   7. concentrate

C 1. feat
   2. competent/common sense
   3. foremost
   4. turned it on its head
   5. extraordinarily
   6. peak

Glossary

A

accelerate (168): to make something happen at a faster rate

accomplished (55): talented

acquire (135): to obtain

agriculture (35): farming and growing crops

alternative (86): something you can use if you do not want to use something else

animated (115): describes films, cartoons, etc., in which drawings appear to move

annoying (67): causing mild anger

appreciation (9): thankfulness for something someone has done for you

associated with (3): connected in your mind with something else

attractive (9): pretty, pleasant to look at

authority (9): an expert on a subject

B

baffle (27): to puzzle

banned (135): illegal; not allowed

belongings (41): the things you own, especially those that can be carried

big hit (106): somebody or something that is very popular or successful

biologist (41): someone who studies all forms of life

blame (148): to consider something or someone responsible for something wrong

brought a halt to (106): stopped

C

calming (67): relaxing

carve (27): to make something by cutting into wood or stone

catch on (78): to become popular

category (122): a group of things that have common characteristics

cause (55): something you believe in and fight for

celebrity (55): a famous person

chain reaction (168): a series of events, each of which causes the next one

character (115): a person in a TV show, movie, book, etc.

charity (55): an organization that gives money or gifts to people who need help

clients (67): customers

come up with (202): to discover something

committed (55): dedicated

common sense (195): the ability to behave sensibly and make practical decisions

competent (202): skilled; having ability to do something

complicated (16): difficult to understand

composer (60): someone who writes music

concentrate (202): to think carefully

confidence (195): the belief in your own or someone else's ability

conquest (161): taking control of a place by force

conscious (161): aware

conservation (161): the protection of things such as wild animals, forests, or beaches from being harmed or destroyed

contestant (122): a person who takes part in a competition

convert (86): to change into something else

convinced (175): sure or certain of something

cooperate (27): to work together

countless (175): too many to be counted

craze (106): something that is popular with many people for a short time

critique (122): to judge the good and bad points of something

cuisine (16): a style of cooking

D

deal (3): an agreement

delighted (60): pleased

descendant (27): a person related to someone who lived in the past

disaster (27): a sudden event that causes serious harm or death

diversity (115): a range of different people; variety

documentary (122): a program that presents facts and information

documents (3): official papers

E

eager (148): wanting very much to do or have something

eliminate (122): to remove from a group

endurance (195): the ability to remain strong even though you feel pain

entice (92): to attract or persuade someone to do something

episode (115): one show that is part of a series

essential (67): necessary

estimated (27): made an approximate calculation

ethnic (16): characteristic of a group of people who have the same culture

evidence (41): proof that something is true

extensive (9): containing a lot of information

extraordinarily (189): extremely

F

fake (92): not real but you think it is real

fancy (161): expensive and complicated

fascinate (35): to interest someone greatly

fatigue (202): tiredness

feast (135): a big meal that celebrates something

feat (202): an accomplishment

figure out (27): to understand, to find a solution to something

flavoring (16): something added to food to give it a special taste

flexible (86): something that can be used in different ways

foremost (189): the most important or most famous

fragrance (92): a pleasant smell

fuel (86): something that is used to provide power or heat

G

generation (16): all the people of about the same age within a society or family

genius (60): great talent or intelligence

give up (195): to stop doing something

grave (175): very serious

H

habitat (168): a plant or animal's natural environment

hang out with (189): to spend time with

heroine (115): the main female character in a book, movie, show, etc.

hoax (148): something that is intended to trick people

horrify (161): to frighten

humanitarian (55): concerned with improving the lives of other people

hung up on (141): worried about something

I

ill (9): sick

illusion (141): something that is not what it seems to be

inspirational (67): making you feel hopeful or encouraged

instead of (3): in place of someone or something

intensify (175): to make something greater or stronger

interfere (122): to be involved in a situation when you are not wanted or needed

intrigue (41): to interest someone a lot, often by being strange, or mysterious

invest (78): to spend money in order to make a profit later

K

kick off (60): to start something

L

lead by the nose (92): to control someone and make them do what you want

legend (148): a story that has been passed down from one generation to the next

link (106): to connect

lively (67): full of energy; stimulating

M

magnificent (27): impressive because of being big, beautiful, etc.

make a mint (78): to make a lot of money

make up (3): to become friends with someone again after an argument

masterpiece (60): an excellent piece of music, art, etc.

microscopic (168): extremely small

misfortune (148): bad luck

mood (78): the way you feel at a specific time

N

notion (135): an idea or a belief

O

on purpose (35): deliberately; not by accident

overcome (55): to succeed in controlling a problem

P

pass up (141): to decide not to take advantage of an opportunity

passed down (16): taught or given to people who are younger than you and who will live after you

patient (67): able to wait without becoming annoyed

peak (202): to reach the highest level

pilot (115): a single TV program that is made in order to test whether people will like it and want to watch more programs

pioneer (189): one of the first people to do something

plain (195): clear and obvious

pledge (175): to promise

practical (78): sensible

praise (60): to express approval

prime time (115): the time in the evening when the largest number of people are watching TV

principle (195): a rule or set of ideas that makes you behave in a particular way

proof (92): facts or information that show something is true

Q

quest (189): a search

quirk (141): an unusual habit

R

ramifications (161): possible results of an action

rearrange (135): to change the order of things

regardless (195): in spite of

remodel (122): to change the style or structure of a room, house, building, etc.

renovated (60): repaired or improved a building, etc.

represent (3): to symbolize or stand for

reputation (148): the opinions that people have about someone or something because of what happened in the past

rich (189): full and productive

ritual (141): a set of actions always done in the same way

rude (9): speaking or behaving in a way that is not polite

run out of (86): to use all of something

S

sacred (161): considered holy and deserving respect

security (135): a feeling of safety

sell like hotcakes (78): to sell a lot of something quickly

sensation (41): something that causes great excitement or interest

shocked (35): very surprised

signify (9): to represent or mean something

silent (27): not speaking; not making any sound

skip (135): to leave something out of a sequence

solo (55): working or performing alone, not part of a group

spark (35): to cause a burst of activity

species (161): a group of animals or plants with similar characteristics that can breed with each other

speculate (35): to guess why something happened

spin-off (115): a show that involves characters from another show

stick to (141): to follow

stick up for (161): to defend a person or a belief

stink (86): to smell bad

swap (122): to exchange one thing for another

system (16): a particular way of doing things

T

theme (115): the main subject of a book, poem, movie, etc.

theory (35): a belief about something that has not yet been proven to be true

tiny (27): very small

tip (78): a helpful piece of advice

toddler (189): a young child

tragedy (148): a very sad event or situation, especially one involving death or suffering

tragic (168): sad, terrible

transmitted (106): broadcast; sent out electric signals for radio or TV

treaty (175): an agreement between two parties

trial and error (106): trying different things and learning from mistakes

tricky (92): difficult to deal with

turn it on its head (189): to make something the opposite of what it was

U

unreliable (9): not trustworthy or dependable

V

vanish (168): to disappear suddenly

vary (3): to differ

vehicle (86): something, such as a car or bus, that takes people from one place to another

victim (55): someone who has been hurt, killed, or affected by a bad situation

violence (41): actions that hurt people or things

vital (175): very important and necessary

volunteer (92): someone who offers to do something without pay

W

weapon (41): an object used in fighting or war, such as a gun

weird (141): strange or unusual

wildlife (168): animals and plants that live in natural conditions

word of mouth (78): passing information by talking about it

Map of the United States

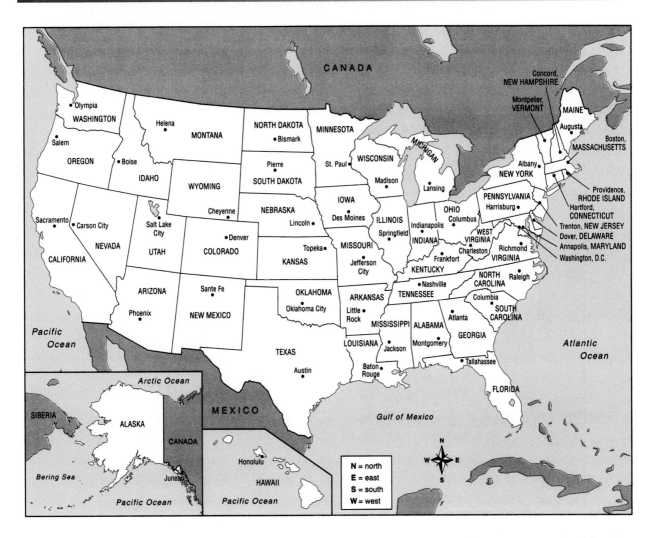

CANADA

Olympia
WASHINGTON

Salem
OREGON

Helena
MONTANA

Boise
IDAHO

WYOMING
Cheyenne

Sacramento
Carson City

NEVADA
UTAH

Salt Lake
City

CALIFORNIA

ARIZONA
Phoenix

Sante Fe
NEW MEXICO

NORTH DAKOTA
Bismark

Pierre
SOUTH DAKOTA

NEBRASKA
Lincoln

COLORADO
Denver

KANSAS
Topeka

OKLAHOMA
Oklahoma City

MINNESOTA

St. Paul
WISCONSIN
Madison

IOWA
Des Moines

MICHIGAN
Lansing

ILLINOIS
Springfield

Jefferson
City
MISSOURI

INDIANA
Indianapolis

OHIO
Columbus

Concord,
NEW HAMPSHIRE

Montpelier,
VERMONT
MAINE
Augusta

Albany
NEW YORK

PENNSYLVANIA
Harrisburg

Boston,
MASSACHUSETTS

Providence,
RHODE ISLAND
Hartford,
CONNECTICUT
Trenton, NEW JERSEY
Dover, DELAWARE
Annapolis, MARYLAND
Washington, D.C.

WEST
VIRGINIA
Charleston

Richmond
VIRGINIA
Frankfort

KENTUCKY
Nashville

ARKANSAS
Little
Rock

TENNESSEE

NORTH
CAROLINA
Raleigh

Columbia
SOUTH
CAROLINA

TEXAS
Austin

MISSISSIPPI
Jackson

ALABAMA
Montgomery

Atlanta
GEORGIA

LOUISIANA
Baton
Rouge

Tallahassee

FLORIDA

Pacific
Ocean

Atlantic
Ocean

Gulf of Mexico

Arctic Ocean

SIBERIA

ALASKA

CANADA

Bering Sea

Juneau

Pacific Ocean

MEXICO

Honolulu

HAWAII

Pacific Ocean

N = north
E = east
S = south
W = west

N
W   E
S

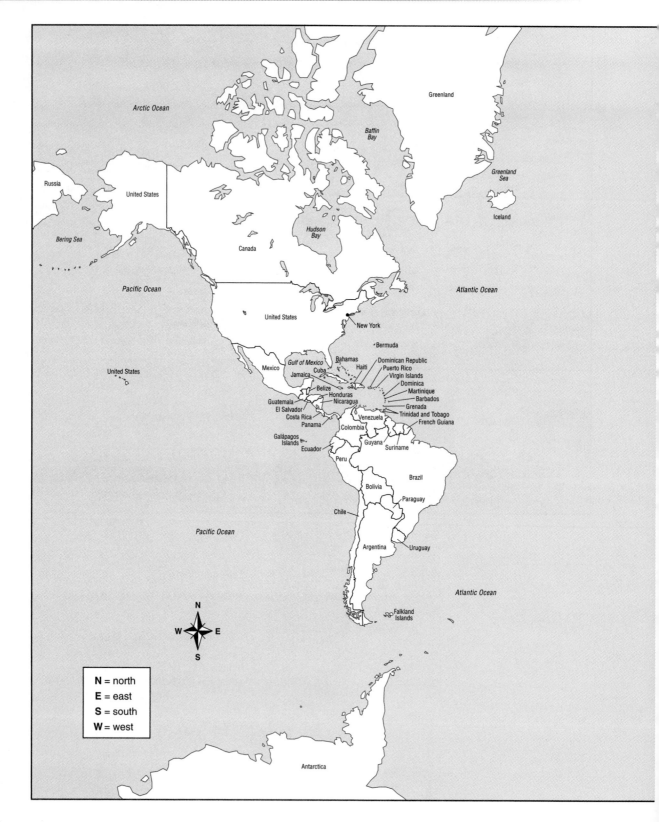

Greenland

Arctic Ocean

Baffin Bay

Greenland Sea

Russia

United States

Iceland

Bering Sea

Hudson Bay

Canada

Pacific Ocean

Atlantic Ocean

United States

New York

Bermuda

Bahamas

Dominican Republic

United States

Mexico

Gulf of Mexico

Cuba

Haiti

Puerto Rico

Jamaica

Virgin Islands

Belize

Dominica

Honduras

Martinique

Guatemala

Nicaragua

Barbados

El Salvador

Grenada

Costa Rica

Venezuela

Trinidad and Tobago

Panama

Colombia

French Guiana

Galápagos Islands

Guyana

Suriname

Ecuador

Peru

Brazil

Bolivia

Paraguay

Chile

Argentina

Uruguay

Atlantic Ocean

Falkland Islands

Pacific Ocean

N
W   E
S

Antarctica

N = north
E = east
S = south
W = west

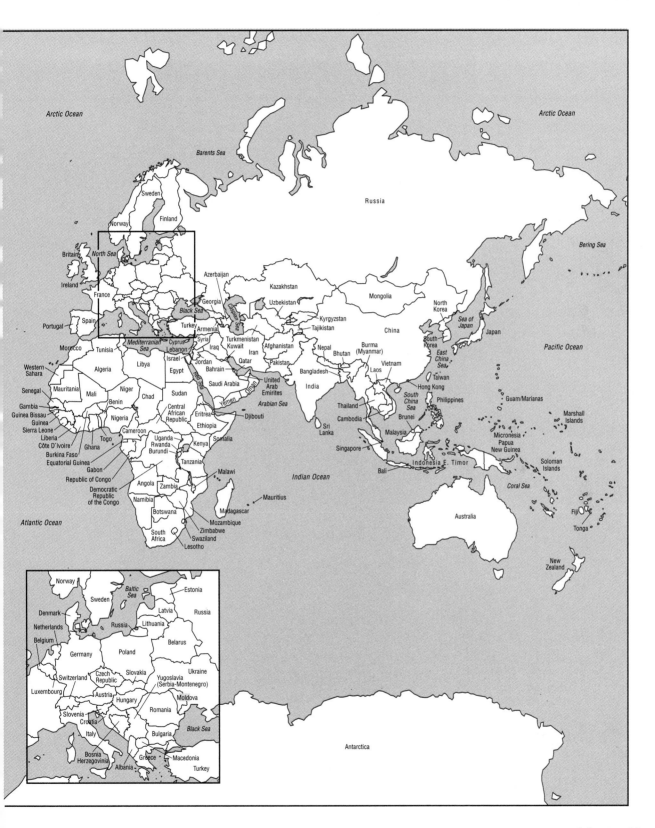

Arctic Ocean

Arctic Ocean

Barents Sea

Bering Sea

Russia

Sweden

Norway   Finland

Britain   North Sea

Ireland   Azerbaijan   Kazakhstan   Mongolia   North
                              France   Korea   Sea of
                                              Georgia   Uzbekistan   Japan   Japan
Portugal   Caspian Sea   Kyrgyzstan   China   South   East   Pacific Ocean
        Spain   Black Sea Armenia   Tajikistan   Korea   China
Morocco   Turkey   Cyprus   Turkmenistan   Sea
              Tunisia   Mediterranean Syria Iraq   Kuwait   Afghanistan   Nepal   Burma
                         Sea   Lebanon   (Myanmar)   Vietnam   Taiwan
Western   Israel   Jordan Bahrain   Pakistan   Bhutan   Laos   Hong Kong
Sahara   Algeria   Libya   Egypt   Qatar   Bangladesh   South
   Mauritania   Saudi Arabia United   India   Thailand   China   Philippines   Guam/Marianas
Senegal   Niger   Chad   Sudan   Arab   Sea
Gambia   Emirites   Oman   Cambodia   Brunei   Marshall
Guinea Bissau   Mali Benin   Yemen   Arabian Sea   Islands
  Guinea   Nigeria   Central   Eritrea   Sri   Malaysia   Micronesia
Sierra Leone   Cameroon African   Djibouti   Lanka   Singapore Papua
  Liberia   Republic   Ethiopia   New Guinea
Côte D'Ivoire   Togo   Uganda   Indian Ocean   Indonesia E. Timor
Burkina Faso   Ghana   Rwanda   Somalia   Soloman
Equatorial Guinea   Burundi   Kenya   Bali   Islands
    Gabon   Tanzania   Coral Sea
Republic of Congo   Malawi   Fiji
    Democratic   Angola   Zambia   Madagascar   Tonga
    Republic   Mauritius
    of the Congo   Namibia   Mozambique
Atlantic Ocean   Botswana   Zimbabwe   Australia
                                 South   Swaziland   New
                                 Africa   Lesotho   Zealand

Norway   Baltic   Estonia
          Sweden Sea
Denmark   Latvia   Russia
Netherlands   Russia   Lithuania
Belgium   Belarus
        Germany   Poland
Switzerland   Czech Slovakia   Ukraine
              Republic   Yugoslavia
Luxembourg   Austria Hungary (Serbia-Montenegro) Moldova
Slovenia   Romania
  Croatia
  Italy   Bulgaria   Black Sea
Bosnia   Greece   Macedonia
Herzegovinia Albania   Turkey

Antarctica

Unit 1   Cross-Cultural Connections

_____

_____

_____

_____

_____

_____

_____

_____

Unit 2   Mysteries from the Past

_____

_____

_____

_____

_____

_____

_____

_____

_____

Unit 3 Music to My Ears

_____
_____
_____
_____
_____
_____
_____
_____
_____

Unit 4 Getting Down to Business

_____
_____
_____
_____
_____
_____
_____
_____
_____

Unit 5 Tune in to TV

_____

_____

_____

_____

_____

_____

_____

_____

_____

Unit 6 Superstitions

_____

_____

_____

_____

_____

_____

_____

_____

_____

it 7 Our Fragile Planet

_____
_____
_____
_____
_____
_____
_____
_____
_____
_____

Unit 8 Living a Long Life

_____
_____
_____
_____
_____
_____
_____
_____
_____
_____